THE BULL IN
THE DARKNESS AND
THE ONE-EYED DOG

Also by Robert T. Sharp, DVM:

No Dogs in Heaven? Scenes from the Life of a Country Veterinarian

THE BULL IN THE DARKNESS AND THE ONE-EYED DOG

Scenes from the Life of a Country Veterinarian

ROBERT T. SHARP, DVM

Essex, Connecticut

An imprint of Globe Pequot, the trade division of
The Rowman & Littlefield Publishing Group, Inc.
4501 Forbes Boulevard, Ste. 200
Lanham, Maryland 20706
www.rowman.com

Distributed by NATIONAL BOOK NETWORK

British Library Cataloguing in Publication Information Available

Library of Congress Cataloging-in-Publication Data

Names: Sharp, Robert T., 1947- author.
Title: The bull in the darkness and the one-eyed dog : scenes from the life
  of a country veterinarian / Robert T. Sharp, DVM.
Description: Lanham, MD : Lyons Press, an imprint of Globe Pequot, the
  trade division of The Rowman & Littlefield Publishing Group, Inc.,
  [2023]
Identifiers: LCCN 2022046102 (print) | LCCN 2022046103 (ebook) | ISBN
  9781493073177 (hardcover) | ISBN 9781493073184 (e-book)
Subjects: LCSH: Sharp, Robert T., 1947- | Veterinarians—United
  States—Biography. | Animals—United States—Anecdotes. | Veterinary
  medicine—United States—Anecdotes.
Classification: LCC SF613.S42 A3 2023 (print) | LCC SF613.S42 (ebook) |
  DDC 636.089092 [B]—dc23/eng/20221017
LC record available at https://lccn.loc.gov/2022046102
LC ebook record available at https://lccn.loc.gov/2022046103

∞™ The paper used in this publication meets the minimum requirements of
American National Standard for Information Sciences—Permanence of Paper
for Printed Library Materials, ANSI/NISO Z39.48-1992.

To Clipper and Homer—
two discarded dogs who went on to influence the lives of so many

Disclaimer

The names of some people in the stories in this book have been changed. Dialogue from as far back as a century ago has been recorded as accurately as possible. Some details are slightly fictitious, but these stories are, for the most part, true.

Contents

Preface

One rainy Saturday morning I wrote a very short story about some drunk hogs. I thought the story was something my great-grandkids might like, and since my wife's into genealogy, she encouraged me to write some more stories. We could include them in the family history. My grandfather was a railroad detective during the Roaring Twenties, but died before I could hear his adventures, and he never wrote them down. He surely had some dillies. So I wrote a few more, just for fun.

I gave these stories to a cat client and friend, Carol Cartaino, of White Oak Editions, to review, and with her encouragement and guidance, I completed a book of tales, *No Dogs in Heaven?* It was published by Carroll and Graf in North America in both trade paperback and hardcover, and was even translated into Czech and published in the Czech Republic in a hardcover edition, complete with humorous illustrations.

Over the years the book has been a source of unexpected fun. I met new people at book clubs and libraries, and enjoyed this new experience, very different from veterinary problem-solving. The book was well received by my clients, friends, and people all over the country, and the pressure was on to write a sequel.

Country Living magazine, published in New York at the time, had just hired a new editor-in-chief, and she thought the magazine needed something different. She read my book, wanted a country veterinarian to write a monthly column, and convinced me that I was just that guy. For the next five years I answered questions submitted from all over the United States in a monthly column called Ask a Country Vet. It was challenging to write, educational, and I met some super-creative young New Yorkers.

But I really liked storytelling, and thought someday I might try it again. However, the practice was growing—we were busier than ever with our son Reid joining me as a second veterinarian, and there always seemed to be more pressing things to do. I had a "day job," and life went on. Writing went to the back burner. I was afraid that I'd told all the good stuff the first time around, anyway.

Maybe not. Not only had sixteen years passed since the publication of *No Dogs in Heaven?*, but one day I also realized that I had "cherry-picked" the stories in that first book from a pretty big cherry tree. It was time to get started on what my clients had been demanding for more than a decade now—Sharp 2.0.

How can a practice dealing with animals for over one hundred years be out of stories? Sooo . . . here are some new examples of why most veterinarians think we have the world's coolest job.

—Rob Sharp

Introduction

I could teach you how to give an animal an injection in under a minute. In just a few minutes I could have you suturing a cut. And if ever there were an easy job, it would be trimming the toenails of a dog. This is pretty basic stuff and so simple that a kid in junior high could learn to do it. What makes it hard are the "complications." I'll give you some examples.

The shot you just learned to give . . . will be in the left eyelid of a 2,000-pound Charolais bull, standing by himself in a pasture. He hates everyone.

The skin you need to stitch is a three-foot cut on the chest of a buggy horse who ran into a wire fence. He's standing in an old barn during a lightning storm at ten o'clock at night. You have to suture by the light of a Coleman lantern since the owner's Amish—no electricity.

And the toenail trim is on Cecil, the St. Bernard. He doesn't like to have his toenails trimmed, and has backed his 150 pounds of growling and drooling opinion into the corner of your exam room. "Come and give it a try!"

A shot, a cut, a toenail trim—all easy, except for a few "complications."

I've heard there's a farm on Peach Orchard Road where everything goes as it should. No complications ever happen there. The farmer calls to make appointments well in advance, and doesn't consider something that has been going on for two weeks to be an emergency. When you arrive, he's there to greet you, and has men to help if necessary. He never expects you to manage alone, or with just the help of his twelve-year-old daughter. His animals are penned up in a reasonable area, and he has a "head gate" built to catch each steer or cow in his corral. Sick animals are in the well-lighted barn, clean, dry, and ready for treatment. He gives medicine until it's gone, and his animals always get well. His dogs and cats are well cared for, have great temperaments, and live to be very old. His horses are gentle and never lame. When you leave, you know that everything will be all right, no one was hurt, and oh, yes, he pays his bills.

I've heard of this farm in the south of Highland County, but I've never been there. "Complications" occur at the places I visit. The first examples I gave are true. Maybe the farm on Peach Orchard Road is just a dream. I'll bet every veterinarian has that dream, and their own "Farm on Peach Orchard Road."

Maybe someday I'll go there. But not today, and certainly not in any stories of this book!

Flying in the Dark

"Experience is what you get when you don't get what you want."

—Randy Pausch

Flying in the Dark

It snowed last night—nine inches down on Marble Furnace Road, but then they always exaggerate the depth down there—anyway, enough to cause the thin ice on the pond behind Lisa Long's dental office to disappear under a white cover. That, of course, caused some dog to run across it, break through, and become trapped in the cold water. Luckily a kid saw this happen, called 911, and the fire department came to fish him out. When he called me the chief said they'd have him out of the water in a few minutes, and could bring him to my office in about fifteen. So I put on my coat, drove over, and parked in the lot out back.

I slid out of the truck and stood there for a minute, looking up into the quiet sky. The snow had stopped but the night air still had that super-crispy feel that lets you know more will come. The clouds were gone and the stars were in the same positions I found them through a sextant years ago. A contrail crossed the sky in the moonlight, but the jet was high enough that you could neither see it, nor hear any sound. For just a few minutes I felt like I could be back up there with them. I'll give you some background while we wait for the fire department and the lucky dog . . .

Night flying is very different—not mechanically but in your mind. It seems quieter, because even though the sound of the jet engines is still in your helmet, radio chatter is minimal. Everything's colored red, because the instrument lights are in red night mode and the rest of the cockpit is dark. You seem to be flying in slow motion as the twinkling towns pass under you. From seven miles in the air, the clear, cold night looks almost ghostly, with stars very visible all around you, and the moon reflected off the wings. For an Air Force navigator who uses spherical geometry and a sextant to find the position of a plane moving at just under the speed of sound, it can be a challenge.

One night our KC-135 tanker was to have a 2 a.m. rendezvous with a B-52 in a dark corner of the sky several hours east over the Atlantic Ocean. We met, the bomber pulled up underneath and behind us, and for twenty minutes we made contact, as fuel was transferred through our boom to the huge jet. The Thunderbirds say they fly a "broom handle" apart at times during their show. We touched. After refueling was done, the bomber dropped back into the dark and disappeared, going off on his ten-hour mission. We flew west, crossing from water to land above New York City at 36,000 feet. At night the lights of New York are quite a show from altitude. From there we passed over Pennsylvania at about 600 miles an hour on a track to Pittsburgh and on west to Columbus. We started the descent checklist and saw the lights of both Cincinnati and Dayton in front of us. Landing at Wright-Patterson in less than an hour, we were on our way to debrief.

Two days later on Sunday afternoon I called my parents for our weekly update and mentioned that we had flown over Niles (my hometown in Ohio) a couple of nights ago. "Did you notice that Frank's started to paint the house?" my mother asked.

She had *no idea* what my job entailed. Not too long after that I turned in my flight suit and put on the white wraparound of a veterinary student, and four and a half years later, I went out into the veterinary battles, and like my mother—I had no idea what my job might entail. You aren't told what to do when a horse gets his legs through a railroad trestle, a cow falls down a well, or a dog gets speared by a hay spike.

After a year of practice in Chillicothe with a great teacher, I bought a practice in Hillsboro, Ohio, from a veterinarian whose father started there as a young vet in 1912. During World War II, when his dad died unexpectedly, the second Dr. Lukhart came home from the Army and took over Hillsboro Veterinary Hospital until his retirement in 1980, when he "sold the joint" to me. My wife Susie and I, and our five-year-old daughter Amy, moved to Hillsboro and settled in a big Victorian house on Walnut Street.

After I'd been in practice for eight years, our son Reid was born, and in 2012—*one hundred years* after Bill's dad started our practice—Reid joined me as "the other Dr. Sharp" and we became a two-man practice with Amy as our office chief, and the heart of the practice. Our clients have known Melissa, our Registered Animal Technician, for over forty years, and many have known the latest Dr. Sharp since the day he was born.

For 109 years now routine, unusual, and sometimes wondrous things have occurred at this practice, and I'm about to tell you some stories of how four generations of veterinarians—two fathers and two sons—dealt with them. A few involve actual medicine or surgery, but many are just those things that make every day unique. So from 1912 to 2021, here they come . . . starting with some stories about a newly hatched veterinarian's early "education."

I'm going into the office now. I think I hear a fire truck pulling into the parking lot!

Riding with Bill

I pulled into Dr. Lukhart's driveway at 8 a.m. and waited while he grabbed his Thermos. It was my first farm call as a practice owner, and Bill said he'd go along for moral support and to keep me from getting lost. The old robin's-egg blue Ford truck with the Bowie vet unit in back had covered the roads and hills of this countryside for over two hundred thousand miles, and it was getting pretty tired. It wasn't fancy when it was new, lacking power steering, power brakes, an automatic transmission, or even a "padded dash." It was a truck, and drove like one—an old one that had been in a head-on wreck on a dirt road just two weeks ago.

"Watch your left foot there," Bill said. "That hole in the floorboard is getting bigger. I thought the last time I drove it home from Jr. Bellamy's that my leg got wetter than usual. The tire throws water up through it when it rains, a real nuisance. The dimmer switch fell through and is swinging behind the tire if you ever need it."

I grabbed the three-foot-long shifter with the big white knob—"four on the floor"—and pressed the clutch down. Reverse gear finally took hold after a few seconds of grinding, and I backed out onto Pleasant Avenue and after a short struggle with the aging gearbox, started in second gear toward the five-point intersection at the end of town.

I had on clean coveralls, a DeKalb Seed ball cap, and a truckload of every drug, instrument, tool, and gadget (including mysterious pole-like pokers) that any veterinarian might need in the field. I was ready.

"Better get gas. That gauge doesn't work," Bill said. Good thing he mentioned that. We stopped at Charlie Greg's Sunoco station for a fill-up and Charlie gave me his card with a phone number on it. "Here, Doc. Bill knows the number already. You're going to need it." He also pointed to his new chrome and violet wrecker that was about as flashy as anything I'd ever seen, and said something I've always remembered. "It doesn't cost any more to go first class, Doc. The payments are just longer." I've used Charlie's philosophy a lot over the years.

We headed south, twenty-two miles to Locust Grove, and Bill said that would be where the back roads got "tricky" and he'd help me from there. It was a warm July day, and a beautiful country drive.

"Now in that barn over there on the left, Marion Michael's place, I got called out to see a sick dairy cow. No one was there, but he said the cow would be in the barn. I looked in and she was in a stanchion eating a little hay he put there for her. Apparently I scared her because she backed up and tore out the stanchion and ran toward the window in the side of the barn and dove through it! How a thousand-pound Holstein could go out a little window like that was news to me. A few minutes later the farmer pulled up and came into the barn. 'Where's the cow?' he said. I told him she tore out the stanchion and went out through the window. 'That's impossible,' he said. Then he walked over and looked out the window. There she was, head down eating grass with the stanchion *and* window frame still around her neck!

"See that little house over on that hill? Grover Frank lives there, and I got called to pull a calf one night. It was coming backward and a real tough job. The calf ended up okay, but a week later I had to go out again, and wouldn't you know it, this calf was coming backward, too. I got it out with some trouble, and as I was packing up my stuff I said, 'Grover, did you have Walt come out and do artificial insemination on your cows?' He said, 'Yes, why?' 'When you see him, tell him to quit putting 'em in backwards,' I said with a chuckle. About a week later I ran into Walt Smith uptown. He's our artificial inseminator for the area. 'What are you doin' telling Grover Frank I was puttin' calves in backward? He just called me and gave me Hell!' Anyway, you'll meet all kinds."

Riding with Bill was a real experience. He seemed to have a story for every farm we passed. "I was supposed to go out to this place we're coming up to here, but they called, and said don't come out, the cow died. Two days later they called, and said they changed their mind—she didn't die, and would I come take a look at her? I asked if she could get up, and he said no, so I told him to prop her up till I got there. I didn't want her to lie with her back downhill or she'd bloat and die. When I got there a few hours later he talked to me a good bit, and we went to see the cow. He had his wife propping her up—she had her back to the barn wall and her feet against the cow holding her up. She was worn out."

We approached Louden, a town with a church and a general store, except the store had been closed as long as Bill could remember. "There's a guy from a couple miles up the road there who may call you. You'll know him when you see him 'cause he walks with a limp. Really a nice guy, raises Nubian goats and sheep. He has a bad limp because one leg is three inches shorter than the other. When he was a kid he fell out of a haymow and broke his leg. His parents figured it would heal, so they never took him to the doctor. It did. Ask him, he'll tell you all about it.

"Serpent Mound right there is a cool place. It's the world's largest surviving effigy mound built by ancient American Indian cultures. You'll need to bring Susie and Amy to see it. One of the worst nights I can remember happened along in here. I was called to treat a cow with milk fever and since my wife Martha had a church meeting, I had the kids. Well back in there, under that high line, runs a branch of Brush Creek. It's worn a pretty good canyon in there, and the back of that field has about a thirty-foot cliff with the creek below it. The farmer—I can't remember his name, it'll come to me—got in the truck with me and the kids. He pointed toward the creek and said, 'She's real wobbly, and back there, Doc. We'll have to park and walk from here, the ground's too soft for the truck.' We started the long walk to the cow, carrying all the equipment I thought we might need, and when I saw her it was obvious she had milk fever.

"So I attached my rope to her halter, pulled her neck around, and then tied the rope to a tree. One bottle of calcium in her vein did the job and she stood up, but staggered toward the cliff and fell over. We hurried and looked over the edge and there she was, swinging by her halter like a big fish on a fishin' line. The rope was still tied to the tree. It took a come-along, three more ropes, a tractor, and an hour and a half to get that cow back up onto the edge of the cliff. We were worn out, and she was too. She collapsed so I gave her another bottle of calcium, and then she got up and walked—right over to the edge and off the cliff again. Harry Sweeney, that's his name, said, 'Let's just shoot her,' but I said nope—we got her up once, we can do it again. Meanwhile the kids in the truck were complaining and it was getting dark. I had a flashlight with me and about the time we got her up again—it took another hour—that light was really dim. Always put two flashlights in the truck—you might need 'em. Anyway we went back to the barn and got the hood of an old Plymouth and put her on it. We hooked her to the tractor and she skidded all the way back to the barn. She looked pretty good after all that. Cows can take a lot of punishment. I called Harry the next day, and he said she was up and eating. How do you write a bill for something like that?"

Locust Grove has an ice cream store and if you're ever there, you have to stop. Bill said so, and we did. The next seven miles went back dirt roads to a place I never found again. When we got to the "farm" where the sick cow lived, it was easy to see why she was sick. An old single-wide trailer with a curved end like they had in the late fifties was the "farmhouse." The "barn" was a garage just about big enough for an old 8N Ford tractor and assorted empty feed sacks. Rusty swing set parts, rusty diesel fuel drums with bullet holes, a few sun-bleached plastic kids' yard toys, and a faded pink flamingo completed the look. In a pen in the front "yard" was a Jersey cow about a hundred years old. She had an udder that almost touched the ground, the teats clearing it by inches, no tail, and graying-tan hair. She stood chewing with a mouth that was so crooked there surely was a serious issue inside.

"Jeff got her at the stockyard sale two weeks ago," the lady of the trailer said. "He got a great deal on her."

All I could think was, *I'll bet he did*. I was afraid Bill might say it.

"What was your plan when you bought her?" I asked. "Were you going to milk her?"

"Jeff thought we could make cheese and sell it. He said it was bringing a high price at the farm market. But she looked bad when he unloaded her, and she's had corruptions in her milk. I told him she was dauncy when he bought her, and she ain't showed no real improvement, but he said you could fix her right up, Doc. Whatta' ya think? She does drink a good long piece."

I felt her udder, and it was hot. The milk was thin and the paddle test indicated a bad case of mastitis, but her temperature was normal. Maybe with some mastitis tubes and antibiotics the old cow might feel better. We talked about getting rid of her milk until the antibiotics were gone, what to feed her, general husbandry, and common sense. We also discussed the fact that she wouldn't give milk forever without having a calf. News to her new owner! Dr. Lukhart added some tips as well. I left feeling we had helped the cow and her owner. Of course we'd have to send a bill "'cause Jeff didn't leave no money."

On the twenty-nine-mile trip back, Bill showed me the trestle where the horse got his legs through the ties, the barn where a cow fell on his helper and almost squashed him, and the sinkhole where he and a farmer spent an afternoon building a tripod out of trees to lift a stuck cow out of the mud—more engineering than medicine.

I dropped Bill off at his house, made it back to the office by noon, and by the end of my first half-day of work, I hadn't brought in a dime. But I wouldn't have traded it for anything. Bill gave me a look into what I might expect in the future, and what fun this addition to small animal practice would be. I didn't expect to do large-animal farm work for my entire career, but maybe for a year, or ten, or so . . .

American Made

I met Guy Kirtland during my first week of practice. Just as my family was about to celebrate Independence Day, which was also my wife's birthday, my home phone rang.

"I hear you're the young vet that's takin' over for Doc Lukhart. Well, I've got an old cow that's down, and I'm not sure why. She just freshened Tuesday and now she won't get up. Can you come down here and look at her? Maybe milk fever."

Right then I'd be glad to go anywhere. I'd just bought a mixed animal practice and wasn't sure I was going to be able to pay the bills. So a call of any kind on any day was more than welcome. The only problem I faced was my lack of experience with cows. Dairy cows were something I'd never planned on dealing with when I was a student. I only paid enough attention in class to pass the National Board Exam. I grew up in a north-eastern Ohio steel town, and when the kids in this area were baling hay, I was using an arc welder in a fabrication plant. The practice I bought was about 40 percent large animal work, but my knowledge of farm animals was quite literally "book learning." I had intended to lean heavily on the small animal side of the practice while I gained some experience on farms. Here was a chance.

"I'll be right down, Mr. Kirtland. How do I get there?"

"Go to Belfast and bear right. After you get to the top of the first hill, my place will be on your left."

"I'm on my way."

First I'd need to find out where Belfast was in relation to Hillsboro. I was told that it was a small village with a gas station that doubled as a carry-out, a feed store, a cluster of small houses, and a church or two about eleven miles south of town on US 73. Once the Odd Fellows had a lodge there, but the building had been empty for years. "I think there's a sign that lets you know you're there, but some kids filled it with bullet holes. You can't miss it, though," said Stan, my next-door neighbor.

Two days after I bought the practice my vet truck, an old Ford F-250 combination of rust and Bondo, was spending time at Charlie Greg's Sunoco Hospital for Dying Trucks. This time it was a tie rod issue, so the truck's front wheels pointed in different directions. I'd stopped at Charlie's, unloaded everything I thought I'd need into an old green Chevy station wagon that would have to do for now, and headed down the "Belfast

Pike," as the locals called it. I needed to learn these names since now I was to be a local.

It wasn't quite as easy as Guy had made it sound, since when I reached the top of the hill there was nothing there. No house, barn, lane, cow, or farmer. This wouldn't be the last time that the directions I got were a little off. What he meant to say was, "At the top of the hill there's a gate in the fence and the quickest way to the barn is to go through the gate and drive across the field until you come to the creek. Turn right and follow the dirt road to the barn, about 100 yards up the creek." I learned all this from a neighbor who had a house I could see, and was home to give real directions.

The old vet truck could have crossed the field easily, but I was in a station wagon and it became apparent that they weren't meant for this. There were soft spots in the field that caused it to sink, and plops of stuff left by cows that burned on the muffler. That station wagon was old, but probably didn't deserve this. It didn't do well off-roading.

When I bounced my way to the barn, Guy was standing there waiting, looking like he'd just left his wife and pitchfork in American Gothic. His cow was standing next to him, apparently waiting as well.

"I thought you said you'd be right down!" said the skinny, wrinkled man in bib overalls. "We've been waitin' here almost an hour. I thought you got lost."

"Sorry, I did get lost. Where's your down cow?" "Down cow" is a term used by farmers and veterinarians, and could describe any number of issues that would make her unable to get up. She could be sick, and just not feel like getting up. She could be hurt from a fall, or have nerve damage from giving birth. Whatever the cause, the longer a cow is "down" the more damage she might be doing to the parts being compressed under her heavy weight. If your leg "goes to sleep" from sitting funny, imagine if you put a thousand-pound cow on it for several days. It's always best to get the cow up and moving as soon as possible. Unless, of course, she is down and resting because she simply feels like it.

"This is the cow," he said. "Funny thing. Just after I called you, she made a few noises and got up! I guess she really wasn't as down as I thought. What is that thing you're driving?"

"Doc Lukhart's old truck is in the shop, and until I get a new one, this may have to do."

At the time, 1980, there were some nice little trucks being built that could hold a special veterinary insert in the bed. These specialized units had refrigeration, running water, and lots of space for drugs, tools, and big obstetrical equipment—pretty much anything you might need in the field. They were designed to precisely fill the bed of each size of truck, including the new small trucks. Gas prices were high and I thought a compact Japanese-made Mitsubishi pickup would be just the ticket. Ford, Chevy, and Dodge Ram only made full-sized trucks at that time, and were gas guzzlers.

"When are you getting a new truck?" Guy asked as I examined his "down cow" to make sure she was okay.

"It may have to be pretty soon. Charlie Greg says he can only hold the old one together for a little longer. The holes in the floorboard are getting worse. Bill put over 200,000 hard miles on it, and it was in a front-end collision just before he gave it to me. The headlights point in several directions, depending on your speed. I've been thinking about one of those compact trucks that get good mileage."

Guy stopped fiddling with the cow, stood up as straight as he could, and said, "Just what nationaaal truck was you gonna buy??"

That came out of nowhere. He apparently knew that compact trucks were all made overseas at that time. Guy was a person who spoke his mind, and had just indicated his disapproval without really saying it. I quickly changed the subject back to his cow.

"I think your cow is a little shaky, Mr. Kirtland. I think you're right that she might have milk fever and I also think she's right on the edge of going down again. Some calcium would prevent a problem later tonight." I gave his cow a bottle of IV calcium, and started packing my gear into the station wagon.

While I was loading my equipment I noticed a flag flying from a pole he'd placed near the barn. It *was* Independence Day, after all. He told me that he'd lied about his age and joined the Marines when he was sixteen— just after Pearl Harbor was attacked. He'd fought against the Japanese in the Philippines, and was wounded in fighting on Corregidor. His son was a Marine and had served two tours as a communications coordinator in Vietnam. He was very proud of him. I told him that I was a former Air Force navigator and had flown missions in Vietnam refueling fighters over their targets. He stuck out his hand, and thanked me for serving—something I had never expected and not something Vietnam vets were used to.

I learned a lot on that Fourth of July call, and my fourth day in Hillsboro as a practice owner. I learned that more specific directions are always good idea, and now I knew how to find Belfast. I learned that you shouldn't take a station wagon out into a pasture. There was a reason why veterinarians who did farm work always drove four-wheel-drive trucks, just like the farmers they visited. Finally, I knew that saving money on gas in a "foreign truck" might be false economy among farmers who prided themselves on patriotism. The next time I was called out to Guy Kirtland's farm I was driving a new Chevy Silverado 2500 4wd with a Bowie vet unit in back. The Chevy looked a lot like Guy's, as a matter of fact. And Mr. Kirtland . . . thank you for your service.

Stone the Perishin' Crows

Halfway between the United Kingdom and Ireland is an island in the Irish Sea. The entire island has a population about the same as Boca Raton, Florida. It's the Isle of Man, and is famous as the place of origin of a breed of tailless cats called Manx. It's also famous for an international motorcycle race held in May or June each year that brings bikers from all over the world to race on the mountain roads of the island. It's considered the world's most dangerous motorsports event by many due to the speed and twisty paths the riders follow. The words "Isle of Man TT" are well known to all motorcycle enthusiasts.

London-born Tom Wilson raced Triumphs and Nortons on the island and other road courses throughout Europe in the sixties when British bikes and their teams dominated the scene. Tom lived in Hillsboro now and never brought an animal into my office that the subject of motorcycles didn't come up. Although he was a lot older now, he still rode fast and enjoyed the fun of two wheels. When I was in high school and college and had that job in the steel mill, I couldn't afford a car, so I bought a motorcycle to get to work. I always had one or more in the years after that, and have a couple old Triumphs and others even now. How could we *not* talk about his racing days? The roads of Highland and Adams County are a lot like the great rolling road courses of Tom's homeland.

When the weather is bad, and the bikes are in the garage, the next best thing to riding is telling stories about riding. Tom's visits were always a pleasure and so when Melissa told me that Tom was coming to the office that afternoon, I was looking forward to a good visit.

"What's the matter with Betty—scooting again?" I asked.

"Nothing. It's not Betty who has the issue," Melissa said. "He's got a goose with a foot problem."

"I didn't know he had geese. Is this some goose he just got?"

"I guess he has quite a few but this one's his favorite. He says it's so lame it can hardly walk."

If I wrote down everything I know about poultry it would fill the back of a business card. Unless you're a poultry consultant dealing with thousands or even millions of birds from the standpoint of flock disease prevention and treatment, most veterinarians don't get to see many birds. A sick bird is a dead bird from an agricultural standpoint. Pet birds are the obvious exception, and really need to be seen by a vet who specializes in bird diseases. It's not that the rest of us don't like poultry—we just don't get much experience.

At four o'clock, in the middle of a misting rain, Tom and his goose pulled into the parking lot. As he opened the door to get out of the truck, the goose and he jumped out together. He didn't mean for this to happen.

He stuck his head in the exit door and hollered, "Robert, the bloody bird's loose!"

I went out the exit door without a coat, and ran behind the pair as they turned the left front corner of the building and headed to the backyard.

Half the fun of owning a goose is watching it run. The big gray guy looked like a World War II bomber on a takeoff roll—wings outstretched, neck extended to the max, big orange bill wide open, tail feathers bobbing left and right in time with the big orange flapping feet. He was covering ground in a hurry, and the sore foot was no hindrance. To perfect the scene, he added a constant rhythmic deafening honk as he ran in front of his owner, almost as if he were laughing.

"He's heading around the back of the office, Tom. Steer him back around the building so he doesn't go straight into the woods," I yelled from the rear pursuit position. Tom ran around to the left and caused the goose to waddle right and around the building.

I circled in the other direction in front of the office to head him off as he came around from the rear. They were running clockwise; I was going counterclockwise. It worked, at least as far as predicting the path of the goose. As I ran around the right side, Tom and the honker were coming straight toward me. Now what?

"Grab him, Robert!" Tom shouted, out of breath and slowing down.

I waved my arms to try to stop him, thinking that if Tom were behind him and I were in front, we could trap him like a baseball player in a rundown at second base. The goose didn't slow down at all, just dodged me and started another lap of the building. We both followed.

"Let's do that again, but this time as you chase him toward me, I'll grab his neck!" Sounded like a plan.

"Right-o."

As the goose and Tom went on their second clockwise lap, I went the other way. The goose appeared on his next lap but Tom wasn't behind him. I let the goose pass me and went to see what was up. I found Tom on the ground, with his right side soaked. He'd slipped on the wet grass.

"Gaw . . . stone the perishin' crows!" he said, whatever that means. "Get a shotgun!"

"Come on, we can get him! Are you okay?"

"Yep, just wet, and getting wetter by the second."

As we stood there in the rain, soaked and laughing, the goose had circled the building and come back around on his own as if to see what happened to us. He held his head high in the air and waddled right toward us. Now was our chance, since we were behind the office and away from the road.

I went around to the goose's right and as Tom went toward him, he turned away and ran directly at me. Silly goose! I grabbed his neck like an axe handle. The honking stopped.

"Great catch, Robert! Hold on tight!"

Tom rushed up and grabbed him around the middle, hugging his wings to his body.

"Let's have a look at that foot while we have him under some kind of control."

"It's his right foot that he's limping on."

"I don't know about you, but I haven't seen a lot of limping going on here."

I looked at the webbing between his toes and saw a little loop of metal sticking out of the tough orange skin of his foot. "Let's go in the office and take an X-ray of his foot."

The X-ray revealed a large fishhook imbedded in his foot with only the loop at the end exposed. I made a small incision over the barbed end, cut off the barb, and backed the hook out by grabbing the loop end and pulling. This was done while Tom held the goose and closed his eyes and the goose honked in my ear.

"I think he'll be okay now, Tom."

"Is this typical of the kind of things you do all day?" Tom asked.

"Sure! We have tomorrow's goose chase already scheduled! Of course not. We see a goose about every other year. Luckily this was just a fishhook in the foot. If it had been something internal I probably would have sent you to see Dr. Carey. He's our poultry expert in the county." (He doesn't know I call him that. It's a good place to refer a goose. He might disagree.)

Melissa interrupted. "Rob, Lonnie Jackson is on the phone. One of the cows took a wrong turn in the barn and came into the side of the milking parlor. She slipped and slid under the pipe rails on the side of the milking pit and is stuck there. Apparently her head and part of her front half is hanging into the lower pit while her hipbones are stuck under the rail. He wants to know if you'll come down and get her unstuck."

"Sounds like a problem, but not a medical one."

"They said they could take a cutting torch to the rail but they're afraid they'd burn her."

Tom was laughing when he heard this. "Sounds routine to me!"

"Why don't you ride down there with me? Your clothes are already trashed from the rain, and you can tell me about your new Suzuki on the way."

"What'll we do with the bird?"

"Put him in your truck. He won't make too much of a mess."

"Gaww!"

"Missy can put him in a cage. No problem. Come on along. It'll be fun!"

And so we left for the farm where nothing goes right. On the way, Tom told stories of the old days of racing when the competitors had no money and slept in tents at the track. Bike parts were swapped between teams. Camaraderie was one of the reasons they enjoyed the sport. There were no million-dollar sponsors or high-tech secrets. Prize money was minimal even if you were a top finisher. Great stories. The trip to the farm was over far too quickly.

I pulled into the barn lot and parked next to the milking parlor door. "Let's go in and see what we're up against."

We stepped over a dozen milk-drinking barn cats and a few odd implements, and went into the parlor. (Tidiness was low on the list of farm jobs at this operation.) The milking parlor was like most in this part of the country. You've all seen a gas station with a pit under the car. You drive the car over the pit and the guy goes underneath to work on it. Well, in this case, four cows walked on each side of the pit, confined on the outside by walls, and inside by pit railings with the farmer down in the pit to wash the udders and milk the cows. Eight at a time was standard. Then when these were done they would walk out the front of the parlor, and eight more would come in behind them, until the herd was finished. This cow didn't come in the front or the back but rather wandered through the barn and then through the room where the milk tank was kept. She recognized her mistake, made a quick turn, and fell down in the milking parlor. Not being one of God's graceful creatures, she slid forward with her head and front half slipping under the bottom rail of the two-rail fence meant to keep cows from falling into the milking pit. She was hanging by her hip bones, scared to death, with eyes as big as oranges. Her front legs were paddling in the air and her head was hanging down into the pit. Stuck.

"Gaww! Blimey!" Tom exclaimed. "I've not seen that before!"

Lonnie came into the parlor, and in his usual good mood said, "What do ya think, Doc? Can we get her unstuck? She slipped in the mud tracked in by all the other cows. At least we got the milking done before she messed things up."

"Have you tried pulling her back up?"

"She don't go for that . . . kicked Leroy pretty hard when we tried. If we can get her down into the pit we can walk her up those steps and out of it. The problem is that she struggles and we need her to hold still so we can roll her on her side and push her into the pit."

"I have just the drug. If she's asleep will she fit under the rail?"

"I'm pretty sure she will. If she won't we'll cut the rail off at the far end with an acetylene torch."

I went back to the truck, loaded a syringe with a little tranquilizer, came back into the parlor, and put the drug in her tail vein. Within a minute she was asleep. Tom and I went on the parlor platform and grabbed her back legs while Lonnie got down in the pit to rotate the front half.

"Watch out she doesn't fall on you if she starts to slide toward the pit, Lonnie."

"I'm a-watchin'."

"Let's turn her sideways." As the big cow rolled on her side, her hips could fit under the rail. All that remained was to move a thousand-pound cow about four feet forward and let gravity do the rest. We pushed. Lonnie pulled. She moved about three inches at a time.

Tom said, "You didn't tell me we'd be pushing cows this afternoon."

"You might not have come along. One . . . two . . . three . . . push!" Another inch. "This is payback for the 'wild goose chase' of a little while ago."

"You ain't from around here, are you, Tom?" said Lonnie, noticing Tom's accent.

"Nope, I'm from Leesburg." Tom winked.

"Quit talking and push. One . . . two . . . three . . . push." Another two inches.

"Blimey . . . she's a bloody load."

All of a sudden, the half hanging over the pit was heavier than the half we were pushing and down she went, falling four feet into the milking area.

"Good thing she's sleeping—that might have hurt. Lonnie, we need to prop her up on her chest so she can burp. Got a bale of straw or hay we can use?"

He went back into the barn and brought out a hay bale, and dropped it into the pit next to the cow. I grabbed her head and pulled it around, while Tom and Lonnie pushed on her neck. The bale was placed behind her shoulder, propping her up on her chest. This was critical so that gas generated in the rumen had a path of escape. We didn't want her to bloat on top of her latest escapade.

"Can you guys get her out of the pit without help once she's awake?"

"Leroy should be back from the stockyard sale in an hour or so. We can get her. Thanks for coming, Doc. She'll thank you too when she wakes up. Nice meetin' ya, Tom."

The trip back to town was filled with cow accident stories. Tom had never been around cattle and enjoyed a few veterinary yarns. His clothes were almost dry when he got back in his truck and said goodbye. As I walked back into the office, Melissa said, "Aren't you forgetting something?"

"What?"

In her best cockney accent Melissa said, "The 'bloody goose' is in a cage in the kennel."

The Smartest Dog

Vicky Valentine was a beautiful border collie. She lived on a farm with several hundred Merino sheep raised for wool production, and it was really fun to watch her in action. Whip-smart, she could move a flock of sheep given hand signals alone. Allen Valentine and his wife had raised sheep for years, but had never owned a dog with Vicky's skill. Border collies are always called the smartest breed on lists made up by "authorities."

About the time I was sitting down to watch *Moby Dick* for the umpteenth time, Allen called. "Rob, it's Vicky. I've hit her with the truck. Can you meet me at the office?"

"Sure. How long will it take you to get there?" This question is mandatory and always asked even if you can make a good guess. It could be three minutes or an hour, and since I rarely know where someone's starting point is, I always ask. Once I was told that it would take ten minutes for the caller to get dressed, another ten to put her makeup on, and then . . .

"About fifteen minutes. I'll have to load her up and then come through town. I'll be there as soon as I can. I really feel awful about this."

I went over to the office and got everything ready to see an HBC. Of all the abbreviations used by veterinarians, this may be the only one universally known: Hit By Car. It happens so frequently that we know in advance some of the drugs and equipment we need to start treatment, and can get it laid out before the animal arrives.

Vicky arrived looking pretty good. She was standing on three legs with scuff marks on her left shoulder. Her gums were bright pink and she showed no sign of shock. Her left front leg was obviously hurt.

"You won't believe how this happened, Rob. I was driving up the lane and she was racing alongside my truck on the passenger side like always. I felt a thump, heard a yelp, and the race was over. Apparently she slipped in front of the tire."

I made sure she wasn't showing any signs of shock, and then took a couple X-rays of her leg. "She has a spiral fracture right across the middle of her humerus, Allen. Here's the drill: We'll give her something for pain tonight and stabilize this. In the morning, if all looks well, we'll give her an anesthetic and surgically place a pin in there. The pin will run the length of the bone in the marrow cavity, and line the bone up and stabilize it. We'll leave a little of the pin exposed under the skin at the top of the bone so we can grab the pin and remove it in eight weeks. I'll want to see her once a week starting next week, and she's gotta stay in the house and be quiet till we take out the pin. No running! Okay?"

"Boy, she won't like that. She's a high-energy dog and keeping her quiet won't be easy. I hope she learned her lesson and won't chase the truck anymore."

"I remember when I bought the practice from Bill I found cherry bombs in the ashtray. I asked why they were there, and Bill said he used them on farm dogs that chased his truck. As he drove up the lane he'd push in the truck's cigarette lighter and when it popped out, he'd light one and hold it out the window while the dog chased him. When the time seemed right, he'd drop it. No dog ever chased his truck twice. It was a little unconventional, but it apparently worked!"

"I guess you had to hope the dog didn't pick it up!"

"Yeah, timing was everything. You didn't want to lose a couple fingers on a slow toss either! Call me tomorrow afternoon and I'll probably tell you to pick her up."

The surgery went well, and Vicky went home the next day to enjoy a couple months of R&R as a house dog. Each week she showed progress, and was putting some weight on the leg by week four. By week six she looked and walked normally, and at week eight we took X-rays and pronounced her fracture healed. While she was asleep we removed the pin. Allen came to pick her up.

"She may act normally, but her leg needs to get a few more weeks of light exercise to be fully useable," I said. "Don't let her overdo it!"

"I won't. I don't want to go through this again. We'll be good. I promise. Why do you have to remove the pin anyway? Can't it just stay in there?"

"Well, it could, but there are a couple reasons. First, a big stainless-steel pin down the middle of a long bone changes temperature faster than the bone. On a cold day, it hurts, and on a hot day it hurts. Humans with old implanted metal bone repairs tell us this. Second, if she should ever break that bone again with a pin down the middle, it will shatter into a lot of pieces around the pin, and that's real trouble to fix!"

"Don't worry, Rob. That will never happen again."

The black and white wonder-dog went home to guide her sheep, glad to be finished with her confinement. I saw Allen uptown one day and he said Vicky was back to her old self—you'd never know anything happened.

Then four months later I got the call. "Rob, this is Allen Valentine. You won't believe this, but Vicky chased my truck up the lane again and I hit her again. I think she broke the same leg!"

"Bring her right in and we'll see."

She stood on the exam table and I felt her left front leg. "We'll get some X-rays but I think she did break the same bone. Just leave her with me and we'll get her fixed up. You know how this works—eight more weeks in the slammer, Allen."

This time she broke the same humerus just below where she broke it last time. Placing a bone pin down the middle of previously healed bone was a little tougher, but I managed to do it. She woke up and went home. I was glad the first pin was out for reason number two—no shattered bone. Eight weeks passed and Vicky was doing really well. I removed the pin and after giving a lecture about dogs and cars, I sent her home to the sheep again.

A year passed. Our daughter was about to leave for college at Miami University, and our son was about to start first grade. We were having a normal Sunday at home when Susie tracked me down out in the garage. "Allen Valentine is on the phone. He won't tell me what's up. He says he has to talk to you."

"I wonder what's up with Vicky?" I went into the kitchen and picked up the phone.

Allen Valentine, in short, sharp, almost furious words, said, "Doc, it's Valentine. Just meet me at the office! This time I want those cherry bombs!" *Clunk.*

You guessed it. Same truck, same lane, same dog, same broken left humerus. In forty-two years of practice Vicky is the only dog I know to have broken the same leg doing the same thing three times. I guess a border collie should hold some kind of record—after all, they *are* the smartest dogs.

Necropsy

Down in the hills past the May Hill church is where you find the turnoff to the Green farm. It's not easy to find, especially at night, because the turnoff is just a filled spot in a ditch and a dirt lane. When I got to know him, I asked Gordon why he didn't even have a mailbox as a marker and he said, "I know where I live," followed by a wink. He and his wife moved from Cincinnati where he'd spent enough years fighting fires that he could retire. He bought 600 acres in Adams County, all hilly with a lot of woods, and raised cattle and sheep. He had some fields where he could make hay, but driving a tractor on some of those hillsides was dangerous. I suppose that after threading a screaming fire truck through city traffic and narrow side streets in the seven hills of Cincinnati, Gordon could handle a steep farm bank.

He asked me to do a necropsy on a cow that had died suddenly. She seemed healthy the week before, but when he made his head count yesterday she was missing. He found her in the woods without a mark on her. Losing one cow was bad enough, but he had others. They say, and I'm not sure who "they" are, that the cow that dies first is always the most valuable. It's because she's the one that can tell you what illness might spread through your herd. She's the "indicator cow."

Gordon and his wife had business in town, and really didn't want to watch me dissect his dead cow anyway. So he gave me directions to the cow, told me where I could find the house key if I needed it or wanted to make coffee, and said he'd call me at the office later. I was on my own. When you do a necropsy on a cow, "alone" is always the way it works out. There's always something that needs done, some emergency, that prevents the farmer from watching. "I'd like to watch, Doc, but I have . . . a Coleman lantern that has a mantle I've been meaning to change. Let me know what you find."

I drove down his lane and parked near the barn. The cow was supposed to be on the other side of the pond, back in the woods about fifty yards, near a big beech tree.

I put everything I thought I'd need in a stainless-steel bucket, put on my boots, and started my hunt for the cow. A couple of coon dogs and a mutt went with me. It was a warm spring day—the pond had already started to get some algae around the edges, and there was a muskrat tunnel near the edge. I discovered this when I stepped in it on my way around the pond, and dumped my bucket full of equipment in the grass. The three farm dogs with me must have thought it was funny. They sat down and watched as I picked everything up and then pressed on.

There were a couple hundred acres of woods crisscrossed with deer and cattle trails on this side of the farm. Some of these trails were as wide as a truck, and Gordon sometimes used them to get into the areas of the farm on the other side of the woods. The cow was near the edge of one of these paths and I found her on her side, as if she'd just decided to take a rest, and did it here.

A necropsy (called an autopsy on a human) on a cow isn't a clean sport. Whatever you've seen on *NCIS* or *Bones*—forget. We're dealing with an 800-pound Hereford-Angus cross that wouldn't fit on Ducky's or Bones' stainless tables. This would be done in the open air, in the position she'd last decided was hers, and then afterward, instead of calling the undertaker, she would have to be dealt with as the farmer chose. No Viking funeral here, and a backhoe was usually involved in the service. I didn't need a scalpel—I had a foot-long necropsy knife and gloves that went up to my shoulders if I needed them. Okay, this is where you, the reader, go put the mantle on your Coleman lantern. Your "need to know" stops here.

The cow died of traumatic reticulitis, pericarditis, and heart failure. She had pulled up some grass with her big tongue and gotten a piece of old fence wire at the same time. Since it was heavier than grass, it dropped from her esophagus straight down into the lowest front stomach of a cow, the reticulum. As the reticulum contracted over and over, it squeezed the wire right through its front wall, poking and scraping the wall of the diaphragm, until it poked a hole here too. What lives on the other side of the diaphragm? The heart, and it didn't like the constant poking it was getting from the wire. It worked as long as it could, and finally quit. This is sometimes called "hardware disease" and is less common since baling wire was replaced by twine. Believe it or not, a finger-sized magnet dropped in a young cow's stomach would usually catch this kind of metal, and hold it in the bottom of the reticulum. It's heavy enough to stay in the reticulum permanently, and prevent trouble for the life of the cow. A few bucks well spent.

Well, I had Gordon's diagnosis but now I had a new problem. Three dogs had been watching, and now they were drooling. They would like nothing better than to dive into a dissected dead cow for a morning treat. They would pull parts everywhere and eat until they were so stuffed they couldn't move. They were dogs after all, not prone to moderation. Neighbor or feral dogs might join in. We could have a fight, injured dogs, and cow parts everywhere. But I had an idea.

I walked back to the truck, and as I suspected, the dogs didn't come along with me. I could see an Allis Chalmers tractor in the barn with a front-end loader on it. I didn't have a lot of experience driving tractors, having not grown up on a farm. Even saying that I had a little experience was an exaggeration. I'd driven a tractor once, but I'd had a lot of forklift experience in the mill. How hard could it be?

I opened the barn doors, climbed up onto the big orange tractor, and looked it over. Nothing too mysterious. Clutch on the left, and two brake pedals on the right, one for each big wheel. Throttle on the column, shift pattern printed on the dash—easy. I didn't really know why there were two shift levers, but I'd try the big one first. I pulled out the choke, pushed in the clutch, turned the starter key, and it fired right up! Hell, yes! I must have found reverse because when I let out the clutch, I was able to back out of the barn. When it seemed appropriate, I shifted into what I thought was second gear (this tractor had a lot of gears), and I was chugging forward at a crawl. I remembered the throttle was on the column. I pushed it upward and now we were chugging faster, and with smoke coming out of the stack. No sweat, this was fun. I made my way around the pond and back up the path through the woods. Those big tires could probably go anywhere.

I pulled up to the cow and a new problem arose. *How does that big bucket on the front of the tractor work?* I played with the levers and figured it out. Now my plan was taking shape. The dogs had already done some damage, but they backed up when "Big Orange" got near. I lowered the front bucket to the ground and on the second try, slid it under the cow. I tilted the bucket back toward me and she slid to the back of the bucket. And for my final trick, I raised her up in the air well above the dogs' reach. I moved the tractor over to the big beech tree and parked it with the bucket up against it. I wanted to take the stress off the hydraulics when I shut off the tractor by letting the tree bear the weight of the cow. Mission accomplished. Almost. *How do I shut this thing off?* I turned the starter key counterclockwise and nothing happened. There were no directions on the dash, even though it had directions for everything else. Don't do this . . . Don't do that . . . Don't put a knife in the toaster—you know. How do you turn off a tractor? I finally decided that if I couldn't shut it off, I'd just kill the motor. I pulled out the choke knob and the motor died in a puff of smoke. Victory.

With their prize out of reach, the dogs followed me as I walked back to the truck. I washed up, washed my equipment, put my boots away, and left for the long drive back to the office. The wild cherry blossoms were starting to be seen everywhere and light green areas were popping out in the woods. Warm weather was on the way and I was glad. Winter is a hard time to work outside.

Gordon called later that day, and I told him what I'd found. While he never wanted to lose a cow, he was thankful no disease was in his herd.

"When I got back, I was afraid someone had stolen my old Allis tractor. The barn door was open and it was gone. I got my backhoe out to bury the cow, drove up and found it. I couldn't figure out what was going on. It was parked with the bucket in the air, and I couldn't find the cow. So I called you."

"She's in the bucket. I didn't want the dogs to eat her and drag parts all over. Maybe it wasn't the best thing to do, but it worked."

"It was a great idea! I'll just take her back to the cow cemetery in the bucket. Thanks for your help on this, Doc."

"Hey, Gordon, how do you shut off that tractor?"

"I always just pull out the choke. Thanks again, Doc."

SOVMA

I'd been the owner of a country practice for only a short time when Dr. Bill Lukhart stuck his head in the back door. "We have a meeting next Tuesday at the Wooden Spoon. I'll pick you up at six." He started to back out.

"Whoa, Bill," I tried to stop him. "What kind of meeting are we going to?"

"The every-so-often meeting of the Southern Ohio Veterinary Medical Association. As soon as you pay your dues you're officially a member. You always want to go 'cause if you miss, you might be elected president. At least you need to go to defend yourself!"

"What happens at a meeting?" This was all news to me but it sounded pretty official.

"We have dinner, talk a lot, and then have a speaker for some continuing education, usually an OSU faculty member. Vets from all over this end of the state will be there. You'll like it."

"I'll be ready. Thanks for the ride!"

Finally a chance to meet other veterinarians from around the area. It sounded like fun but a little intimidating. I was sure all these experienced guys would look at the newbie with "that look." It might be the place to learn practical methods of dealing with large animals not taught in school. I actually looked forward to it.

The big night came, Bill was on time, and we headed off to the Wooden Spoon. As you might guess from the name, this was a restaurant that was dark brown simulated logs on the outside, served "home cooking," always smelled like fried food, had a frayed plastic menu that was rarely used because everyone got the buffet, and was packed on weekends. If you haven't been there, you've been to a clone. I loved it.

It was easy to see we were in the right place since the parking lot had a row of pickups with fiberglass vet units in the bed lined up on the side of the building.

"I see Lightner's here, there's his red truck. Bob Moss is parked next to him in the old Ford. Doesn't look like a big turnout. I guess some of these guys are still getting crops in. Petersen in Chillicothe plants about 600 acres and I know he's still running beans at night."

"It never occurred to me that some vets farm. When do they get time?" I asked.

"Well, a lot were farm boys who grew up, went to college as Ag majors and then went on to vet school. They worked the farm with their family and some still do, or they inherited it. Echlander over in Circleville has a couple hundred head of Angus and about a thousand acres to worry about along with his calls. He probably won't be here."

We walked in, turned left, and headed toward the meeting room, away from the rest of the restaurant. It was a nice warm room with a fireplace actually burning wood, a speaker's podium at one end, and tables that could hold probably seventy-five people. Tonight there would be about twenty-five, so we had plenty of room to spread out. Cigar smoke, pipe smoke, and fireplace smoke were the atmospheric specials that night. Every veterinarian wore either a flannel shirt, coveralls, bibs, or western wear of some sort, with pointy-toed cowboy boots, engineer boots, or just ankle-high boots. String ties were held in high regard, the ones with a turquoise and silver slider. Carhartts hung on pegs. No one could tell the new guy in a white shirt, tie, and sport coat.

"Let's go over here in back. I hear the speaker tonight is Dr. DeVine from OSU and her subject is acid-base balance in fluid therapy. She won't hear us snore back here." We sat down at a table for four, were joined by two other guys with the same idea, and my continuing education began right away.

"Boys, this is the sucker, I mean the gentleman, who bought my practice. This is Dr. Sharp. He spent a year doing small animal work over in Chillicothe with Jim Wilson. I don't see him here, by the way. Anyway, he used to be in the Air Force and has a wife and a little girl." Bill turned to me, "I can't say anything nice about these two so I'll stop right there—Dr. Moss from Bloomingburg and Dr. Lightner from Lynchburg." End of intro.

Dr. Moss lit up his pipe, Dr. Lightner lit his cigar, and I didn't have to light anything, being able to inhale enough smoke just sitting there. Someone hit a glass with a spoon, announced there would be no auxiliary meeting since no wives were present, and tonight we would all be eating from the buffet compliments of the treasurer of the group. Everyone stood up and emptied the room like a fire drill. You didn't want to be last, I was told. They'd be out of pickled beets.

You never want to eat near a veterinarian if you're bothered by indelicate talk. Dr. Lightner started the indelicacies while he enjoyed his first piece of fried chicken.

"Boy, I had a bad one this morning. Joe Semple, down near Emerald off Pine Top Road, had a big Hereford have her calf last night. It was a bull calf and huge, but she got it out okay. She and the calf wandered downhill a little ways and she fell down on the gravel near the edge of the pond that

Joe built down there. While she was lyin' there I guess she felt the urge to push again because she did . . . and out came her uterus into a pile of dirty gravel and manure."

As an aside . . . a prolapsed uterus is one of the more challenging problems of bovine practice. Getting a calf out is sometimes a difficult, multi-hour veterinary project, but after the big baby is out, the cow sometimes blows the uterus inside-out through the same birth canal and there, hanging behind her, is a huge, red, soft, bleeding mess of an organ that needs to go back home quickly. Dr. Lukhart once described replacing a prolapsed uterus in a cow as "trying to push a bushel-basket full of Jell-o through a keyhole." It was a messy problem, and one disliked by most vets.

Dr. Lightner continued . . . "Now I not only had the uterus to deal with, but also the contamination of gravel and manure. I was afraid she'd get an infection we couldn't control, but Joe said she was a good producer and he wanted to save her. 'Pull out all the stops.' So luckily I could get the truck down near her, and my water tanks were full. I gave her some of that new tranquilizer that Jeff Storm's been selling for Butler to get her to stay still, and slid a tarp under the uterus, cleaning off the big pieces of gravel as I went. Once the tarp was under it, I got my hose out and rinsed and scrubbed till all the manure and stones were off." He started his second piece of chicken. "This is good tonight!" he added, holding up the drumstick. "I used almost all the water in my tank but I'm pretty sure I got it cleaned well enough. The water was cold so that helped shrink the membranes a little. Then I sprinkled it with 'shrinking dust' [sugary powder to reduce swelling], put on some new sleeves, and after about twenty minutes of wrestling, got everything back where it belonged. I put in a couple of stay sutures and loaded her with antibiotics. Blew the whole morning. Then I had to reschedule everything."

"That's nothing," Bill chimed in. "Mossy, tell Rob about that one you had a couple years ago over by the state park. That one was a classic."

"Wait just a minute, fellas, I'm getting some more beets from the buffet." He was gone and back shortly. "Well, I got involved in about the middle of this situation, but I'll tell you what I learned after I pulled up.

"The Harringtons had a dairy operation over on the North Swamp Road. They milked about eighty head at any given time, and the dry cows stayed in a lot right up next to the barn. It had been a rainy spring and the fields were soaked. The dry cow lot was drenched and the rain continued with no end in sight. Todd called me and said he had a cow with her uterus out and would I come and get her fixed up. I told him I'd be there as soon as I could, but that I had a stop on the way to deliver some mastitis meds at another place. When I pulled into the barnlot I saw a ten-foot pile of wet cow manure with a Holstein's head sticking out the top, mooing like an air-raid siren. I stopped, went over to Todd, and said, 'What the hell, Todd? How'd this happen?'

"So Todd started his story. It seems the ground was too wet to get a spreader out in the field, so Todd used a scraper on his tractor and moved all the manure that accumulated on the concrete pad into one huge pile so when the rain stopped he could get rid of it in short order with his front-end loader. The cow had her calf and popped her uterus out, and was lying down in the rain on the concrete. She wouldn't or couldn't move. Since Todd wanted to move her into the barn for me, he had a great idea. He wrapped a rope around her horns, passed it through a block and tackle and up through the pulley at the peak of the barn—the one they sometimes use to lift hay. He would lift her up a foot or two, and swing her gently into the barn, letting her down on some clean, dry hay."

"That was the plan. For power he would hitch up a harness mule that they used to pull a small cart at fair time. Sounded good. He rigged up his apparatus, passed it up through the pulley and down through the brass fixtures on the mule's harness. The mule took up the slack and Todd was admiring his ingenuity when his Redbone Coonhound came full-tilt around the barn chasing his daughter's favorite cat. The pair ran behind the mule, spooked the hell out of him, and he took off with the cow attached. She rose up off the ground and was lifted vertically until the block and tackle hit the pulley at the top of the barn. Then, of course, the rope broke and the cow was dropped tail-first into his ten-foot manure pile, and there she was when I pulled in.

"So I said to him, 'Okay, Todd, what's the plan now?' Well, it worked once (sort of) and he thought we could lift her straight up out of the manure mountain, hose her off, and get her in the barn with the same apparatus as before but using a tractor for power this time. The mule was fired. And that's what we did. It took several hours to get her into the barn and clean, and then I went to work. Her uterus was pretty easy to replace, and I left enough antibiotics to keep the inevitable uterine infection from killing her. She was lucky the fall didn't hurt her. She was up in the air almost to the second floor of the barn when she was dropped. Anyway, I saw her a few weeks later and she was milking fifty pounds a day. Tough ol' cow."

It took a while for us to quit laughing and then Bill said, "I love that story. Did I ever tell you guys about the cow that went down with milk fever in the pond last year? It happened down past the church at Pricetown where the old feed mill used to stand. For some reason nothing goes right at that place, and I dread the calls from those boys. Rob, you can have 'em now! Do you suppose we have time for dessert? I'm kinda full but I hear the apple pie here is number one. Anyway, Charlie called—he's the oldest of three brothers—and said they had a cow down with milk fever. No sweat, right. When I got there he pointed to the pond and said, 'She's out there, Doc. Sorry.' Well, no one mentioned this on the phone.

"'Do you want me to put on my water-wings to treat her, Charlie?' I asked him, but he said they had a plan—like your client, Mossy! They brought a big old Allis-Chalmers tractor with a front-end loader on it down to the pond and said, 'Get in the bucket, Doc, Randy will drive you out. It ain't too deep. You can treat her from the bucket.'

"Of course I thought they were nuts, but I got a bottle of calcium, an IV line, and some needles, and climbed into the bucket. Randy lifted me up and started chuggin' down the bank with that ol' scoop bouncin' with me in it. I didn't really worry 'til he went into the pond and the front wheels started to sink in the mud. 'No problem, Doc. We're doin' great!' Randy said. Bullshit. He wasn't in the bucket. Luckily the cow wasn't far out and the pond was pretty shallow. Still, only her head and neck were above the waterline. I reached over the side of the bucket, found her jugular, and put in the needle. She never moved an inch. You know how you always hold the bottle below the cow's back so the calcium doesn't run too fast? I couldn't do that, since her back was underwater, so I had to kink the line after I attached the bottle. It ran in okay and didn't kill her. I signaled Randy to back the hell out of there, and let's see how she reacts. He raised the bucket and me (just to be ornery, I think) high in the air and backed that ol' orange tractor out of the pond. He lowered me and grinned. 'I told you it would work!'

"Before I could say, 'She isn't up yet' . . . she was up and started to head for the bank. I was worried that the effort would put her down again so after she was on dry land, I roped her and put in another bottle. Who's going with me to get pie?"

I had the feeling that these three guys could go on all night, and frankly I wished they could. But just after the trip to the dessert bar, the Carousel projector was set up and our "education" began. Acid-base balance in fluid therapy is really important, but not something anyone wanted to hear that night. Oh, we all pretended it was great, and applauded when it was done, or maybe just because it was done. Anyway, Dr. Adkins from Chillicothe missed most of it, slumped in the back corner. He had the best seat, dark and far away.

I couldn't wait for the next meeting. I'd learned a lot, knew what to wear next time, and couldn't wait to ride in the bucket of a front-end loader. Besides, they'd be electing a new president at the next meeting. I had to go to make sure it wasn't me.

A Morning's Work

"Have you ever noticed that there are people who do things which are most indelicate, and yet at the same time—beautiful?"

—E. M. Forster

A Brief Warning

The young veterinary student stood behind a beautiful chestnut colt in her crisp new coveralls with a knowing smile on her face. You know she had to be a *real* student because she had a stethoscope resting around her neck like a TV doctor. The pair was standing in a pretty grass pasture dotted with wildflowers. This is the picture of what veterinary life is like on the cover of the pamphlet you might get if you asked a college of veterinary medicine for admission requirements and school literature. This is a lot like the photograph of the Marine, standing rapier straight in his perfect dress uniform, white gloves, and belt, exemplifying what it's like to be one of the few and proud.

Both pictures might be accurate and true. But if you ask a Marine who was on Iwo Jima or in Afghanistan or the old veterinarian trying to get a hundred-pound calf out of a crazy Charolais cow crashing around in a field, they might tell you it's not quite like the pamphlet cover. We have a picture in our mind of certain jobs and it's usually painted in the best possible light. Veterinarians are usually seen with a cute dog on the exam table, or a track horse standing still while the vet listens to his heart.

This brings me to the point. I was told by a city friend that my job is "gross." I've had clients tell me they would rather see their pet put to sleep than have . . . an amputation for example, or a nasty wound repaired. It might be upsetting to a human, but to a dog or other animal, it's just something to deal with that calls for some adaptation—and then they wonder what's for dinner? They don't think about it. To a veterinarian, it's a problem to be solved and like the animal that has the problem, it's never "gross." I'm only warning you here because you, like many people, might think that veterinarians pet clean dogs all day and have no trouble at all, or like the student with the chestnut colt, just stand there with a stethoscope and a smile. You might think some of the stories that follow are indelicate or gross. To those who fix problems like these, they are just daily experiences and a challenge to repair. They're just cases I thought you might like. So read them with this in mind—it's just another day at the office.

Clipper

We all called her Big Alex even though her name should have been Tiny Alexandria. She had a granddaughter named after her who went by Alex, but since we couldn't have two, Grandma was the "big" one. She weighed about a hundred pounds and didn't deserve the prefix, but she didn't care, so we always referred to her as Big Alex, and she was our county humane officer—big in heart, work ethic, and courage when necessary.

"Can you guys help me here?" she said as she carried the lanky, mud-covered, muzzled dog in the back door of the office. He was slipping out of her grip and heading toward the floor. "This is an abused dog that I finally confiscated. I threatened to take him for a long time, but this was the absolute end. He's been running loose and lives in an abandoned car. He's in really bad shape now, and needs some quick attention or he's gonna die."

"Why's he muzzled, Alex? Is he ferocious?"

"Naw. He's wearing the muzzle 'cause he's chewing his skin off. You won't believe this by lookin' at him, Doc, but he's a purebred Standard Poodle. I took him to the groomer to get him cleaned up, and when they started to clip they found somethin' that you need to see."

He slipped out of her arms and onto the floor scale, which registered forty-six pounds. His hair, from head to toe, was several shades of mud brown and knotted into mats that were inches thick. Too weak to stand, he was carried over to the treatment table. Under the tangled, wet mats we could see a barely breathing dog with eyes that were sunken and painfully dry. The wet mats extended down his legs to giant pads of flopping feet. His tail was a stiff cord of tangled dead hair and mud. I peeled back the small place where the groomer had started to clip and underneath I could see skin—red, wet, and infected, technically called a moist pyoderma. In this infection, shimmering like rice dancing in a hot frying pan, were a million maggots. The smell was stomach-turning. It takes a lot to make the people who work in a veterinary office nauseated but this had crossed that line.

"Oh, Alex. We need to give him an anesthetic right now. No wonder he's chewing his skin. It's alive. Aww, he's beyond miserable. Does he still have an owner that we need to deal with?"

"Not any more. He's a confiscated dog now. We've notified the sheriff and this case will end up in court. This woman was raising Labradoodles, and needed Pierre twice a year to breed a Lab. The rest of the time he slept in an abandoned car behind a shed and had a horse for a friend. Her Lab is going with me to the shelter. She's as big as a house, filled with pups. Just try something, Doc. I know he looks bad, but he's really a nice guy. I saw him last year when he wasn't as bad off and he was actually pretty affectionate. The scary thing is this woman has kids. I wondered how they were being treated, so I alerted Human Services. That lazy woman shouldn't be taking care of anything."

"He looks like if he had a vote, Alex, he'd want to call it quits. He's in horrific shape, and probably won't last the day. Maybe we should just . . ."

"I know, but if he lives he might be worth it. If he dies, we tried. You may end up having to put him to sleep anyway."

So we tried. I thought the anesthetic would kill him but he struggled along. We clipped every filthy hair down to the skin, and by the time he was waking up, we'd freed up his face, neck, and most of his sides back to his pelvis. After we clipped the hair, we washed his skin with antibacterial soap, and killed the swarming mass of maggots as we went. It was apparent that underneath this smelly mess was a skeleton of a dog. But he woke up and ate a little. Maybe he was going to die . . . but not today.

We gave him IV fluids, antibiotics, vitamins, anti-shock drugs, and anything we could give to keep him from dying. After three more days and four more anesthetics, we had freed his legs, feet, and tail from their hairy sleeves. He now resembled a skeleton with hairless, red, infected skin stretched tightly over it. His left rear leg had been broken and healed with a large knot, and his jaw was slightly misaligned. Old injuries. He was still too weak to stand, but he could wag his tail. He looked like a piece of Halloween art with a battery-powered rear end.

After a week of treatment, he could stand with help. After another seven days, he could walk across the room. His skin had been damaged so badly by the infection and maggots that black dead patches would appear. I peeled off these areas of dead skin while he stood and wagged his boney tail, never offering a complaint. By week three we had to anesthetize him one more time to do some skin repairs, sliding nearby healthy skin over large areas where dead skin had been removed. He woke up, looked at us, and wagged his tail.

He liked to walk outside when he could, and looked forward to his trips around the yard. Some hair was regrowing in patches, and Big Alex was amazed at his progress when she stopped to visit him. After five months he looked like a shaggy, off-white dog with a few hairless areas, tall, long, and very happy. He weighed eighty pounds now, having gained thirty-three pounds during his recovery. When he sat on the floor as I stood next to him, I could pet his head without bending over. He liked it, but if you gave him a toy, he'd lay it down. If you gave him a treat, he'd spit it out. These were all new things to an unsocialized dog and he didn't know what to do with them. He was more than a little backward from his two years of neglect. Since he didn't even know his name, we changed it. He just didn't look like a Pierre.

You could say we named him Clipper after the most sleek and graceful of all sailing ships, or after the PanAm Clipper, one of the most beautiful of all transpacific aircraft. Or you could say we changed his name to Clipper after the five clipper heads we ruined getting rid of his mud-covered mats. It didn't really matter because he liked it, and when you said it, he wagged his body. Clipper!

"It's been five months now, Doc, and this dog's still freeloading here. I can take him back to the shelter, and try to find a home for him," Big Alex said on one of her visits.

Clipper didn't know a lot, but he knew one thing—I was his friend. It would break my heart to send him away now. I took the step. "Alex, I think he's found a home, if you're okay with it. He can come home and live with us."

Big Alex looked at him and then at me and said, "I knew that. I was just hoping you'd say it."

So Clipper came home to live in a house after spending his life in a car. He learned to live indoors and eat regular meals and act like a house dog, a really large one. His splotchy hair, some short, some long, still made him look like a stray. He walked into our house, looked around, found his favorite spot, and curled up like he'd been there since a pup. He was home.

You would think it would be hard to housebreak a dog who'd never been in a house. Why wouldn't he just "go" anywhere he got the urge, since that was what he was accustomed to doing? You'd be wrong. Professional dog trainers will tell you that a dog learns to use one particular type of surface (this is called "substrate preference") as the place to "do their business" and we all hope, as we house-train a dog, that preference will be grass and not an oriental rug. Clipper had always been on grass, never anything else, and so his substrate preference was built in since birth. He always waited to go outside and never made a mistake. As time went on, the whole family began to say that Clipper could get away with anything because I thought he was "perfect."

The first time we took him to a groomer was quite an experience for him. He'd never seen or felt an electric clipper running since he was asleep during all his clip jobs, and he was apprehensive. He stood on the table like a stuffed toy and looked sideways at his groomer, Steph. He never moved, if you don't count shivering, and when he was done, the hair on his face and feet was clipped poodle-short and his body looked like cotton candy. With a pompon on his tail and the top of his head, he was a full-fledged foofoo dog! He actually wasn't white at all, he was "light apricot," and now looked like a show dog—nothing like the dog Alex carried into the office. His transformation was complete. He was incredible.

It was almost unfair to take Clipper to school on career day. The guidance counselor learned that if you invite a vet, he'll probably bring a dog. Twenty-five tables were set up in the gym, each with a local businessperson there to describe what it's like to be a lawyer, a fireman, a funeral director, or an accountant, and at one table, a veterinarian with a huge apricot poodle that is all fluffed up—"Who let this happen? All the kids are over at his table! Why does he get to bring a dog? You're cheating, Sharp!"

I wrote a book some years ago, and when I was asked to talk about it at book clubs or libraries, I would always ask if I could bring my dog. After I promised that he'd be good, they'd hesitate, but give permission. Clipper was always well behaved. He'd wander around the room during the meeting and put his big soft head on each lap, waiting to be petted. He moved slowly, never licked anyone, and was always a gentleman. When the petting stopped, he would simply move to the next person.

When I was done with my book talk, I would ask if I could tell a dog story, and I told the story of Pierre, the neglected dog, and how he'd been treated, and his recovery. When I mentioned that the humane officer volunteered to find him a home, and paused for just a minute, it didn't matter whether I was in a classroom of kids, or a living room full of book club wine drinkers. Someone would always ask, in a quiet, almost apologetic, quivering voice, "Did he find a good home?" People, kids or adults, had no idea that Clipper was that dog. When I answered that, "He never knew his name so we changed it to Clipper, and he has his head on your lap," the response was predictable and always the same—a gasp followed by tears and tissues. This reaction was then followed by the reason for telling this story, "Maybe your next dog could be an abuse case, or from a shelter."

"Right to Read Week" is an annual school event with library programs and speakers. For several years I was asked to take part and read to the kids. The marquee in front of the library on Main Street always read "WELCOME CLIPPER" and underneath in smaller letters—"and Dr. Sharp." He became a star. In an auditorium full of kids, he never minded when a second grader wrapped her arms around his neck and kissed him. His message to kids wasn't a plea to adopt an unwanted dog, but something much more basic. "I knew that Clipper was going to be my dog when he had no hair and his skin was covered with sores. We were friends, and you don't pick your friends by how they look."

Over the years, he proved to me that he was the one and *only* dog I have ever known that could be trusted in any situation. Older folks and nursing home residents loved him because of his patience and his non-threatening demeanor. Who's afraid of a big dog in a poodle costume? Kids even half his size loved him, because kids and dogs have a kind of secret language that he understood. For those of us lucky enough to enjoy the company of dogs daily, it's easy to recognize when a special one comes along.

I once was asked to talk to a gymnasium full of high school kids about careers in veterinary medicine. I took Clipper, and finished with a dog story—the one you just read about Pierre. By the time I was done, Clipper had worked his way to the far end of the gym, being petted by front-row kids all the way. A student raised her hand and asked just one question: "Does he do TRICKS?" I walked away from the microphone and in a normal voice called, "Clipper." As the gym full of kids watched quietly, he left the young girl who was petting him and slowly walked the length of the gym, like a model on a runway, and came over to my side, sat down, and looked up at me. That was his trick. He was my dog . . . my friend. People say Clipper was lucky to have survived. I was the lucky one.

Hard-Luck Sam?

Night phone calls are never good. It doesn't matter what your job is, a night call usually means bad news for someone, and it might be you. It was bad news this time for a pup, as Mike Williams was calling near midnight.

"Doc, my puppy just got into rat poison and I don't know what to do!"

"What did she eat, Mike, was it d–CON?" I asked, half awake.

"It wasn't d–CON. It was some new stuff I got at the feed mill. It was a one-pound bag of Black Death pellets that I got to put around the corncrib. She ate almost all of it!"

"Read me the label." He tried, but his pronunciation was close enough that I knew what he meant. Good news—it was an old-style anticoagulant poison for which we had the antidote— provided we got to her in time.

"The first thing we need to do is try to get the poison out of her. Did Mary eat it?"

"Nope. This is a new German Shorthair pup I just got. I'm hoping Mary can help train her. She's just eight weeks old and weighs about nine pounds. I've only had her two days."

A nine-pound dog ate a pound of rat poison—not the best situation. It must really taste good, or this pup was starving. "First, Mike, give her enough hydrogen peroxide that she vomits most of it back up. Give her a tablespoonful and wait a couple minutes, then do it again, and again until she vomits. Then bring the bag of poison with what's left in it to the office with the pup. It'll take you about ten minutes to get her to vomit and twenty minutes to get here from New Market. I'll meet you in a half-hour or sooner." I wanted to read the bag myself.

I got dressed, went downstairs quietly past the sleeping "guard poodle," and drove to the office.

I was waiting when Mike and the poison-eating pup arrived, and gave her an injection that makes a pup throw up anything remaining in even the vicinity of the stomach. I followed up with an injection of the antidote and some pills to continue for the next three weeks. I wanted to see her again in a week to check her clotting time, but I thought she'd be fine.

Samantha (or Sam if you weren't mad at her) grew up to be a great bird hunter. She loved to hunt and point, and she loved to retrieve. So it didn't come as a surprise when she retrieved a rubber ball shot out of a toy gun by Mike's little boy. Except she brought the ball back in her stomach, instead of her mouth. We had X-ray proof. There it was, and now, about a year after she ate a pound of rat poison, I was going to have to retrieve the ball myself—surgically. If there's such a thing as a favorite surgery, retrieving a foreign body is one of mine. When you're holding the ball, or the toy, or the battery, or the Christmas decoration in your hand, you know the problem is solved. It's like a treasure hunt for the cure! I found the ball in Sam's stomach and within the hour she was waking up from surgery. I sent the ball home with her to a happy family.

I saw her for her annual exam and vaccinations later and Sam looked great. She'd put on a little weight and looked like a mature German Shorthair now. Her abdominal scar was barely visible and she was becoming the best hunting dog Mike had ever worked with. And then she was hit by a truck.

"Doc, I hate to call you this late, but I let Sam out to go to the bathroom this evening and she didn't come back. I went out to look for her and a guy in a pickup truck was down at the end of my lane. He was all upset 'cause he'd hit a dog. It was Sam. She's still alive. Can I bring her in?"

"You bet. I'll be waiting at the office when you get there." I could be at the office in about seven minutes, so I had time to get out all the drugs and equipment I'd need to treat her for shock if necessary. It doesn't matter what's broken or what's bleeding if you don't get an IV line in place and treat for shock quickly. Bleeding is obvious and can be seen, but shock, low blood pressure, rapid heartbeat, and poor perfusion (pale gums) are common when 5,000 pounds meets 60 pounds. I was ready when she arrived.

Mike carried her in. We put in an IV catheter and started the fluids quickly. She was indeed shocky, so all the usual drugs were given, and while they were taking effect, I examined her.

"Can she stand, Mike?"

"When I got there she was just lying in the ditch with a glazed look on her face."

As I felt around on her body it was obvious that she had a broken left femur and a broken left humerus. She wouldn't be able to stand on either left leg. Later X-rays revealed that her pelvis was broken in several places as well. She had probably been driven over.

To give you the short version to the finale, she responded well to the shock treatment and was pretty much out of the woods the next day. I anesthetized her, and using intermedullary pins (rods in the marrow cavity) and wire, repaired the long bone fractures. Her pelvis would heal on its own, and with a little help she could stand in a few weeks. Good home nursing care was critical. After eight weeks her bones were healed, so the pins were removed. Six weeks after that, she was on the trail of pheasants in South Dakota.

Since she loved to retrieve and loved to chase balls it didn't surprise me when Mike called again one day. "Hey, Doc, remember that ball you removed from Sam? I think you'll need to do it again."

"No way! Surely not!"

"We can't find it and Caleb and Sam were playing with it in the yard."

"I'll take an X-ray, but I'll bet not. It's in the yard!" When I was a student I watched a surgical resident open up a bulldog, performing a C-section, and was surprised to find that the chubby dog had no pups left in her uterus. She'd only had one, and it was at home. He should have taken a look before surgery. I don't do surgery on dogs who "might" have a foreign body. X-rays were taken and there it was. Same damn ball. Rubber ball surgery 2.0 was about to start.

"I'll get it out, but this time I'm keeping the ball, Mike!"

I followed the still-visible scar line from a couple years ago and voila! My old friend the rubber ball was out and on the counter. Recovery was uneventful and the ball went into an office drawer.

When Sam was seven she was brought into the office yet again. "I have no idea what's wrong with her," Mike said. "She got up this morning and had trouble walking. She didn't eat anything and just shivers."

"Was she okay yesterday?"

"Yep. We hunted over her in Fallsville woods most of the morning and she was fine. Today it's like she's wore out. Can't hardly move."

I examined her from one end to the other. Nothing was obvious. Her temperature was normal. Her lungs sounded normal, and she had no obvious wounds. But I had trouble examining her mouth. She wouldn't let me look. She stood on the table and seemed unable to relax. This wasn't like Sam. She had spent more time in my office than most dogs, and she was always hyper-energetic and very agreeable. To stand on the table and not move, and to not open her mouth to let me have a look, was a puzzle. I drew blood from her. In those days it took a day to get the results, so I kept Sam overnight.

Her bloodwork was unremarkable when it arrived by fax. What could make a dog not want to move, stand stiff as a sawhorse? And then, just like a TV detective who has a revelation, I had a diagnosis! Sawhorse stance and a mouth that wouldn't open—locked shut. Lockjaw! The old name for tetanus. We've all heard of it, but it's rarely seen. How rare? In forty-two years of practice I have logged in only two cases, and Sam was the first. A bacterium, *Clostridium tetani*, is a non-air-breathing bug that gets carried deep into a wound and produces a toxin to which different species of animals have different sensitivities. Horses are so susceptible that we give them tetanus toxoid annually to prevent problems, and antitoxin if they get a wound of any kind. Birds never get it. Humans get a tetanus shot once every ten years and dogs don't get vaccinated at all. It's very rare in dogs and cats.

I called Mike and gave him the news. I didn't know the prognosis, but I'd try my best. I called every "horse doctor" in the area and rounded up all the tetanus antitoxin they could spare. I spoke with a bacteriologist at Ohio State about which antibiotic to use. And while all these drugs were taking effect, it occurred to me that I would need to find the source of the puncture or cut. I ran my hands over every millimeter of Sam's stiff body and on the inside of her left rear hock I felt what I thought was an abnormal bump. I gave her a local anesthetic, cut over the bump, and there it was! A half-inch piece of a twig had been driven into her leg. It was so small that the resulting puncture didn't even bleed, but it was big enough to carry in the bacterium that caused the problem. With the wood removed, the antibiotic dealing with *C. tetani*, and the antitoxin handling the poison, I told Mike that we had every reason to think Sam would be okay. She was.

Years later, against all odds, Sam died in her sleep of natural causes at the age of fourteen. I occasionally look at that ball in the drawer where all my weird souvenirs are kept, and think of her. One of my favorite dogs, and one of the luckiest . . .

Making Hay

White Dog lived on a farm down the road about a mile from our office. He was a shepherd mix. The Shelby family planted corn and soybeans on most of their farm, except for one field where they cut and sold timothy hay. White Dog was one of those dogs who just showed up one day and hung out on the farm. He loved to be with the head of the family, Dan. He slept on the porch, went out to the barn with Dan, followed the Gator out into the fields, and generally acted like he belonged. Dan didn't mind, and actually liked the company on his daily chores. One creative moment he gave the white dog a name: White Dog.

If you drove by the Shelby farm in late spring you could see huge round bales scattered all over the eighty-acre hayfield. This is simply where the baler dropped them during the process of making hay. At other times you could see them lined up in rows, all gathered up and neatly arranged at one end of the field. How do you move a one-ton large round bale from where it fell out of the baler to where a truck could pick it up? Dan used a hay spear attached to the front-end loader on his John Deere tractor. This spike, over three feet long, could be stabbed into the center of a bale, so that it could then be lifted and carried by his tractor.

He'd already moved half the bales from the front part of the field and put them where they could be loaded on the tractor-trailer for transport to a large cattle operation. He drove over to a bale a little farther away with White Dog following close behind. Sometimes little critters would come running out of the bales when they were moved, and White Dog loved to chase them. This was a day of real fun for him. He'd never miss it. Dan aimed at the end of the big bale, lowered the spear, and drove forward into it. He heard a yelp, looked around to see if the tractor had driven over White Dog's foot, didn't see anything, and pressed on. When he lifted the bale he looked, and all of a sudden felt sick. Between the tractor and the hay bale was White Dog, speared like a tomato on a shish kabob and hanging off the ground. The spike went in his left side behind his ribs, and came out his right side in about the same place, and on into the hay bale. Dan thought White dog was surely dead, but he was still moving, so Dan pulled out his cell phone.

"Doc, if I bring White Dog in right now, can you see him?"

"Why? What happened?"

"I'll be there in five minutes. He's been stabbed." End of call.

Dan was there before I could tell Melissa about his strange call, and he carried White dog, whining, to the treatment area and put him down on the stainless table. "Oh, Doc, I put the hay spear in one side and out the other. He's gotta die. No way he can take that."

White Dog's color wasn't bad, but his heart rate was rapid and irregular. We clipped his front leg, started an IV, and gave him the drugs for shock. Surprisingly he wasn't bleeding as much as I would have expected.

"If we're going to save him, Dan, I'll need to give him an anesthetic, and go in to inspect the damage, stop the bleeding, and do whatever I can. But I'm afraid you're right, he probably is going to die."

"Go ahead. I'm going home to sit down. I feel sick. Let me know as soon as you know something, Doc."

"I'll call you," I said as the big man left for his truck.

We quickly clipped and cleaned the symmetrical wounds on his sides as the IV fluids were running, and when he was ready, anesthetized him and prepped his abdomen for an exploratory. I felt like this might be a necropsy, just done a few minutes *before* he died instead of after.

As I made the midline incision on his abdomen, I expected and was prepared for blood to come pouring out. It didn't. I enlarged the incision and could hardly believe what I was seeing.

The spear had missed the spleen, and on its way to the other side had pushed the slippery intestines out of the way without harming them. It had gone behind the liver and stomach—no damage there. It missed the pancreas, and it missed a whole list of blood vessels that were all large enough to have names. The kidneys were untouched and if I were to sum up his injuries, I'd say that other than a piece of grass I found stuck to the greater omentum, White Dog was perfect. Well, there was that hole in each of his sides, but nothing internal. What were the odds of that happening? We flushed out his abdomen in case any other contaminants had ridden in on the spear, and closed him up. I put some staples in his spear holes and called Dan.

"Well, he isn't dead," I said. "In fact, aside from my incision and a couple of holes in his side, he's fine. He was shocky, but we've stabilized him, and he can go home later this afternoon. He's waking up now, and frankly I can't believe it."

"You know, maybe I should rename him Lucky. What do ya think, Doc?"

If he changed the dog's name, neither I nor the dog ever knew it. He still always responded to White Dog and chased Dan's tractor for ten more years. The scars on his sides were light brown, and proof to anyone to whom Dan told his story.

So now, when I drive by Dan's farm, and see the big round bales all lined up in a row, I always point to the place, and say to the person riding in the truck with me, "You won't believe what happened to a white dog who lived on that farm . . ." I still don't.

K-9

"Dr. Sharp, this is the Hillsboro police department. We've had an accident with one of our cruisers and we wondered if you could come to the scene and give us a hand?"

"Sure, where?"

"The cruiser's on the Willettsville Pike, at the turn in the road by the library. The officer has been taken to the hospital and they need you at the scene."

"I'll be there in five minutes." I wondered what had happened and why they needed me. Maybe the officer had swerved to avoid a dog, and wrecked, or hit a dog and wrecked, or hit a deer and wrecked. Anyway, the crash scene was in town just a short drive from my home, so my questions were answered quickly.

"Glad you're here, Doc," said the sergeant in the road. "Officer Carey was responding to an emergency call out by the lake and hit this curve too fast. The cruiser went in the ditch, Harry got shaken up pretty badly, and a squad has already taken him to the hospital. But when he hit the ditch, Barney in the back there got thrown against the barrier. He must have hit it pretty hard 'cause there's blood on the partition. Can you take a look at him?"

"I'd be glad to. Can we take him over to my office?" Barney, of course, was a "K-9 unit."

"That's the problem. We can't get him out. He's way in the back there, and he's pretty mad. He doesn't know who did this to him, but I think he's blaming us. The last fireman who tried to grab him backed out of there quick and said Barney wasn't having any of it. He knows what a dog can do. We thought maybe he'd let you grab him."

Grabbing a dog that's been trained to attack might not be such a great idea. I knew Barney, and his forte was drug sniffing. He always was a gentleman at the office, so I opened the door, sat on the floor of the back seat, and we had a discussion. "Did those mean firemen in the big suits try to hurt you, Barney?" (Right now I was sounding like the old woman in sunglasses who tries to convince her Pekingese that the bad doctor didn't mean to hurt Snookums with that big needle.)

"Come here, Barney, and let me see your boo-boo." It's not really what you say, it's the way you say it. My mother told me that so many times it stuck. Barney didn't have a clue what I was saying, but he knew me, and he knew I wasn't going to add to his bad night. After a couple minutes, he came over and put his bloody nose on my leg. I scratched his head for a while and hooked up his lead. We went to the office in my truck and fixed his "boo-boo." Nothing serious. Harry was released from the hospital the next day and picked up his K-9 unit. The cruiser got the worst of the crash.

You watch these dogs on TV and hear stories about their remarkable tracking and sniffing ability, but one night I got a front-row seat. I was sleeping when the phone rang.

"This is Jackson Security. We have an alarm drop at your office. We've notified law enforcement and they will meet you there."

I put on some clothes, went out to my truck, and left for the office. No one was on the street at 3 a.m. so I could drive as fast as I wanted. The police wouldn't stop me, since we were going to the same place. When I pulled in, a cruiser was waiting and Officer Bob Reynolds was walking around outside. Bob was a trapshooter, and we'd shot at the state shoot and other competitions together. We were friends. We walked around the building and found a broken window. We entered the building, I turned off the blaring alarm siren at the code box, and we looked around. No one was there, but apparently when the siren went off, the burglar dropped his Corona bottle, and ran for the nearest exit. He couldn't get out since the door had a keyed deadbolt, so he climbed out the window, the way he came in, leaving the place smelling like beer from his broken bottle.

Officer Reynolds called the P.D. and another officer came out in his special cruiser marked (you guessed it) "K-9 unit. Stay Back." Another client, Officer Rick Sewell, and his dog Bronco got out. Bronco was a Belgian Tervuren, who was trained in tracking, drug detection, and suspect apprehension. He was a wonderful dog, friendly with schoolkids, and the best tracking dog in his class at training. He loved to follow a scent, and if necessary he could bring down a bad guy. This was his night to have some fun and shine.

Rick walked him by the window, waited while he picked up a scent, and off they went. He wasn't tracking the Corona delivery truck at the local carryout either. Bronco sniffed the ground and went out of our parking lot toward Route 50. He went west, toward Producer's Stockyard, and two blocks later went into their parking lot. Can you imagine how many smells there are in the parking lot of a stockyard that handles thousands of cattle and hogs every year? Bronco pressed on through the lot and then north, back into the woods. Five hundred yards into the woods he made a right turn, then headed through the woods again, east toward Hillsboro. He went behind a Certified gas station and onto the sidewalk where he continued in the direction of town. About a half-mile later he made a turn south and crossed Route 50 again and followed the trail through a backyard. He was in a residential area now and could walk on the sidewalk. He did, and fifteen houses later he ran up to the front door of a small white house. Rick knocked on the door, a sleepy man answered, and said only he and his brother lived there. His brother, it turned out, was hiding under a blanket on the couch, with muddy shoes and a penitent look. Bronco had led the police *right to his door.* You can't do better than that.

One last quick example . . . the police had chased a suspect from the place where he was seen burglarizing a business to a construction site a block away. They knew him and knew he was often on drugs and unpredictable. They saw him run into a portable toilet to hide so they surrounded it. This was New Year's Eve, by the way, and traffic in the area was heavy. When they called the man's name, he opened the door to the plastic potty and said he had a gun. If they tried to come after him he'd shoot one of them or maybe himself. They called for Bronco.

Rick and Bronco arrived at the scene, walked toward the blue toilet, and Rick said, "C'mon, Frankie, do you really want to die in a plastic outhouse on New Year's Eve? Just come out. You know everything will be okay if you do."

The man said he would rather stay in there and die.

"If you don't come out, the dog will come in. He's not afraid of being shot."

Rick gave the command to Bronco to alert. Prepare for attack. Now Bronco's heart was never really into attacking or biting, but his preparation for it was superb. He lowered his head, the hair stood up on his back, he bared his teeth, drooled like a rabid dog, snarled, and lunged at end of the lead. Then he watched as Frankie the Doper threw out his gun and exited the toilet without incident. I asked Rick later if he would have really sent Bronco into a portable potty after a guy with a gun. He said he knew he wouldn't need to. Bronco can scare the ---- right out of someone.

Police dogs are invaluable members of law enforcement. We sometimes see a story on the news about a K-9 unit who died on duty, and how hundreds turned out for his funeral. In the group somewhere will be his partner, a cop who lived with him, fed him, played with him, took him to work, and just like us, cried when he lost his best friend.

Signs in Sinking Spring

I'm sure there's a story behind the name "Sinking Spring" but that could be for another day. Let's just call it a small village at the southeast corner of Highland County, as far away from the sheriff's office as any place could be. They have a mayor, a couple of stores, a gas station, some churches, and a lot of peace and quiet. A good place.

A horse needed to be castrated in Sinking Spring and I was the veterinarian to do it. Mary Jane Davis asked me to come to her parents' small farm on Saw Mill Road to geld Stoney, a quarter horse that she wanted to break for trail riding. She said he was a little "green," but she could handle him. Words like "green," "spirited," "spunky," and "peppy" all mean the same thing—trouble. I much preferred "well-trained," "tired," "old," or "worn-out" if I had to pick a favorite horse adjective. I liked thirty-year-old former parade horses that would let you approach in an empty field, rub their neck, draw blood without fastening a lead shank, and would still be standing there when you walked away. That's just the opinion of someone who *always* has to press on the part of a horse that hurts.

I showed up at the house at nine that morning and met Stoney, who stood like a gentleman in the field next to the house. He let me run my hands all over his body for a quick inspection, look in his eyes and mouth, and generally give him the once-over. Nice young stallion.

"What do you think of him, Doc?" Mary Jane asked.

"Frankly, I thought he'd be a little harder to handle. He's really going to make a great trail horse. Have you been training him yet?"

"Every night. He learns fast too. I agree; he's a winner. I really like him!"

I went to the truck, got drugs, a lariat, a bucket of warm water, and some other needed equipment and put it on the ground near Stoney. Then I told Mary Jane how I expected to do the surgery. I wanted to do the job with no help, just for safety's sake, but she was welcome to stand back and watch. I wanted her to know that a sleepy horse might move quickly and I wanted room to work. In the meantime a neighbor in his seventies or eighties walked over and sat down in a chair on the lawn a little distance from us.

The first drug was given in the jugular vein and Stoney never moved an inch. He lowered his head, and I gave the second drug and in a matter of a few minutes Stoney wobbled a little, and was gently putting his half-ton body down on the grass. I placed him in a position where I could do the job, scrubbed him, gelded him, and before you could say, "Boy, this is going well!" he was starting to wake up. I kept him down till I thought he was awake enough to stand, and then, with the help of the lariat, guided him to his feet. Voila! This could have been a video for classroom instruction. All the things that could go wrong didn't! There was no bleeding, no swelling, no injury, no rodeo, and frankly if every horse castration went like this, I'd be very happy.

When I was done the old guy sitting in his lawn chair arose, and like the great prophet himself, made his way slowly over to where Stoney and Mary Jane and I stood. He pulled the pipe out of his mouth and finally spoke. "You know why that went so well, don't you?"

What do you say to that? I could have said "skill" or "experience" or "modern drugs" or any one of a lot of good answers, but the best thing I could come up with was . . . "Why?"

"The signs were right."

Of course. What was I thinking? I wondered . . . if things had gone to hell, the horse had gone crazy and crashed through a fence, the incision bled like a fountain, the results swelled up as big as a cantaloupe, and nothing went right, would that be *my* fault or would the signs get the credit? I bet I know.

The signs he was talking about, of course, were the signs of the Zodiac, and the practice of "moon farming" and the mix of the two as they relate to the parts of the human body. A popular picture in almanacs as early as the 1800s (and publications before that in the 1700s) showed a drawing of a man with the signs and dates of the zodiac pointing to certain parts of his anatomy. The phases of the moon played a role here too, because waiting for an *annual* zodiac change took too long. For example (without trying to explain the fake "science" behind it), the moon could "bring blood" to certain areas of the body, and operating on those areas at this time and date would obviously cause hemorrhage. When the moon is in Leo, you better not be castrating a calf or big trouble was on the way, and that was a proven fact since the heart was affected during this time. All this baloney was questioned by 1850, but just in case it might be true, it's still in print *today*. Check it out for yourself. I was just lucky enough to geld Stoney when "the signs were right."

I went back to town to ask Bill Lukhart about this. "Of course," he said. "One of the most annoying situations I ever encountered was a farmer down in Berrysville who would only cut pigs by the signs. Lifting up 100 pigs weighing twenty pounds and castrating them is tough work, but when you have to wait for the signs, and the sign isn't right until they've fattened up to fifty pounds, it makes the job a lot tougher. The farmer knows better, but just in case . . ."

I went to our weekly Rotary meeting several months after that and sat next to one of our prominent citizens. These are great meetings and we learn a lot from the programs about a variety of subjects. Ours is an old and active club with a huge budget and a history of charitable giving. If you need something done, ask a Rotarian.

As the meeting was about to close, Harry, the man next to me, turned and said, "Well, Doc, I took the big step. Janey's been after me for a long time and I finally called Dr. Johannsen. I'm gettin' a vasectomy next Friday."

I wasn't sure if I should say "congratulations," or "good luck," or whatever might be the proper response to a statement like that, but I didn't have to say anything. Harry said something next that left me speechless.

"He wanted to do the surgery when he had an open appointment last month, but I had him wait. The signs weren't right. You can't be too careful!"

A Dog, by Any Other Name . . .

The bloodhound puppy sat on the exam table and looked up at me as I listened to his heart. He looked like a kid wearing his older brother's clothes. His skin was so loose and soft that you could grab a handful anywhere and lift it straight up six inches. His ears hung all the way to the table and his lower eyelids already had that sad "ectropion" droop. The rest of his face was made up of lips, large and swinging, that undoubtedly moved up and down with those ears as he "ran like the wind" after some puppy prize. All leading to, of course, the world's greatest sniffer.

I looked at his records and started to write when I noticed something—he had a terrific name—Mudflap! I stopped writing, and said to the proud new owner, "I love your puppy, and you've found the perfect name for him. How long did you think about names before you settled on Mudflap?"

"About as long as it took to watch him come in from the yard with his droopy parts covered in mud. Then he shook, and all of that skin and mud went in different directions."

It made me think about names, and some things I've noticed about them over the years. This is all just my opinion, and you can disagree, but I'll share it anyway.

People rarely tell you their pet's name without telling you who came up with it—like it's not their fault. "His name is Raynaldo. My son named him after some comic book guy."

"His name is Anton. I can't tell you why my wife thinks that's a good name for a Lab. It sounds French to me."

"His name is Armani. My daughter says he's very stylish. I wouldn't know."

I find myself doing the same thing when people ask about our office cat. She was dropped off with a large skin wound that the owner said had "been there for years." He wanted her to be euthanized since it wouldn't heal (by itself, apparently). We asked if we could try to repair her wound instead of putting her to sleep, and he said, "She's all yours. Her name is Panther." Can you guess what she looks like? Now, after her long recovery, Panther cruises the office and acts like we work for her. I guess it could be worse—she could have been named Blackie. I know the selection of a name, and what constitutes a good one, is entirely in the ears of the listener, but I still say when asked, "Her name is Panther. She was named before we knew her," and I now have done the same as everyone else. We could change her name, I suppose. She wouldn't pay any less attention.

This business of giving credit (or blame) to someone for an animal's name dates back a long way. Consider *Latrodectus mactans* (Fabricius, 1775) or *Homo sapiens* (Linnaeus). Scientific names are always given in Latin, genus first, then species, with the credit for that name following, usually parenthetically. Carl Linnaeus was the originator of binomial nomenclature and gets more than his share of credit for a lot of names, so much so that his name is frequently just an abbreviation—*Canis familiaris* (Linn).

We all know that our animals have more than one name. Cattle are sometimes identified by ear tags. Ol' Number 77 or Moonpie, as this cow was sometimes known, was famous for being rideable. Our neighbors registered their German shepherd as Smithfield's Magnus von Tadsen with the AKC. They call him Magnus, and when they want him to come in from the yard they yell, "Noochi, Noochi, Noochi, Noochi." Three different names. Most of the more grandiose names end up being shortened in actual use. Thus the Kentucky Derby winner Rich Strike becomes Richie to his friends, and a striking Manx cat named Penumbra is called Umby by members of his family. One of my favorite horse patients was a huge palomino quarter horse named William the Conqueror. When he was young he would be decked out in silver parade tack and lead a big city Thanksgiving Day parade, strutting his stuff with his rider carrying the American flag. I bet he was an impressive sight! He was old when I met him, and grazed on forty acres with his pasture pals. When it was necessary to examine him, he would only come to you if you carried an apple and called him by his preferred name . . . Bill. He would come running toward you and pull up six feet short, refusing to come the rest of the way. If you turned your back to him, he would come and rest his huge head over your shoulder, waiting for his apple—a game Bill played for years. William the Conqueror! You may know another palomino named Bamboo Harvester. Maybe you'd know him better by his other name . . . Mr. Ed.

Scientific names are rarely used but most living beings, plants included, have multiple names as well. For example, who says, "Watch out! There's a *Latrodectus mactans* (Fabricius) in your shower!"? We would probably say, "Watch out! There's a spider in your shower!" Or the truly detail-oriented among us would say, "Watch out! There's a black widow in your shower!" All three names are correct and get the point across. If you saw her daily, you could give her a fourth name: "Watch Out! There's Beulah again!" We sometimes trip over the scientific name of an organism or the disease it causes, and so we change it to something simple—a common name. For example, the human and animal disease borreliosis, caused by the bacterium *Borrelia burgdorferi*, is finally just called by the name of the small town where it was first discovered—Lyme, Connecticut—Lyme disease.

Food names are held in high regard by some. Amy's kept a list of patients named after food, just for fun, and to date we have over 135 different examples. Many, like Muffin and Oreo, are picked a lot, while others, like Basmati and Beignet, are singular examples. Lady Godiva, Jellybean, Kumquat, Fruit Loop, Pickles, and Whiskey (the diminutive of the more formal Whiskers) are patients. When a litter is born and it's decided that they're all so cute that—why not, let's keep 'em all—everyone in the family gets in on the naming and each member names one pup. It's how a litter of Dobermans were named Moonbeam, Sundance, Starlight, Elsa, and Frank.

Some names are really trendy depending on current movies, like Bella from *Twilight*, Copper from *The Fox and the Hound*, and *Frozen*'s Elsa. Or some are named after sports figures who will be forgotten by the time the dog is ten years old. "Apparently he was named after some football player. I think he played for the Bengals."

For five years I wrote a monthly column in *Country Living* magazine. Questions were submitted by readers, and each month we selected some and gave answers. One person asked, "I read that naming a cow will boost her milk production. Is it true?" Absolutely. A British study demonstrated this. The more kind and calming personal contact a dairy cow has with her farmer, the more she milks. Of course they have names just to keep records but talking to her, calling her by name, and playing soothing music will prevent cortisol production, which inhibits milk letdown. To say it in a few words: they become contented cows, and give more milk. President Taft had a cow that grazed on the lawn of the White House and provided milk for the family. Her name was Pauline Wayne.

Science aside, all of our animals need names, and picking an appropriate one is tougher than you'd think. I believe it should be unique, descriptive, not screamingly obvious, and it should project something you wish your pet to convey. For some examples of the obvious, what breed is Tyson? Winston? Angus? Hershey? Pierre? Oscar? Snoopy? These are such obvious names that everyone uses them. Boxer, bulldog, scottie, chocolate lab, poodle, dachshund, and beagle, in case there was any doubt.

While some people go with the obvious, others come up with one-off creations. Fatty McButterpants is a favorite cat patient. Pepper was named for his spotted coat but after he'd gone to obedience training, he graduated as Dr. Pepper. We see one of his academic colleagues, but this one's a cat named Dr. Micro-panther. If you get a pair of pals, consider the names of some of our patients: Cheese and Crackers, Tater and Tot, Peanut Butter and Jelly, or my favorite duo—Scar and Tissue. I have no idea where that came from. We also see Big and Fat, but that's *one* cat who is neither big nor fat. In forty-three years of practice, I've never seen a Fido, a Rover, or a Felix, and those names are famous, at least in cartoons. I've also never seen a cat named after any of the cats from the famous Broadway musical of the same name. But I know Hambone!

A friend has a beautiful male Siamese cat, and they picked the name Shesahe (She's a he). Picture this—"Aww. What a pretty kitty! What's her name?"

"Shesahe."

"What's *his* name?"

"Shesahe." Now the thinking begins . . .

Some names have no explanation. One of our patients is a huggable old pug with a chubby body and a loving disposition. Over the years his chronic eye problems have left him with a saggy wink. We all love to see him, and he returns our greetings with whole-body wiggles. Who would guess his name would be Viper?

Animals learn their names through repetition. You can call your dog the Polish word for footstool, and if you use it enough, he'll know you mean him. For many years we shared our office with a cat named Claude (or was it Clawed?). He was missing a rear leg and was always in trouble. He would run across the room and leap up and hang from my back with his front claws digging in while I was doing surgery. When I had bills to pay or taxes that were due, I'd place the paperwork in neat piles on the floor of my office. He would sneak back and shuffle them like a pile of paper litter. He liked to come into exam rooms and torment dogs. I'm sure for most of his life he thought his name was Dammitclawed. But he was an affectionate cat and we loved him, even if he liked to bite a little. Our clients were amazed at his ability to jump with a hind leg missing, and he served as a good example of adapting to a disability. They all loved him too, even if he liked to bite a little . . . when they weren't looking. Dammitclawed!

Soooo . . . I'll leave you with this last thought. Pick a name for your pal that you won't be embarrassed yelling at the top of your lungs when he sneaks out of the yard. Pick a name that won't require you to say, "My granddaughter named her." And pick a name that . . . *if you were that dog*, you wouldn't have to hang your head, and say to the new dog next door, "Hi Twinkie! I'm Pope Michael the Eighteenth. My dumb owner named me."

Fore!

No one makes an appointment for an emergency. They just appear. Since you never know when an emergency will occur, you could have more than one to deal with at once. That happened one snowy December afternoon.

We had Magnus, the German shepherd, on the big treatment sink, since he'd had the bad judgment to run under a four-wheeler after a squirrel. The four-wheeler was going about twenty-five miles an hour at the time.

Juggernaut James the bulldog was being held by our high-school assistant, over on the surgery table. His X-rays showed a urethral stone that had kept him from urinating for the past two days. He sat, like all bulldogs do, with a worried look on his face.

And now Patsy Moore just arrived with her three-legged yellow Lab named Bruce, who was shooting bloody diarrhea from his south end like the water cannon at a gold mine. Good thing there were only three people in the waiting room, here for scheduled appointments, or I'd be running late.

It's always best to prioritize emergencies—triage, as they said on *ER*—so let's see . . . who's first? Since bloody diarrhea is sometimes contagious, we put Bruce on a thick stack of blankets in the isolation room for now. James the bulldog was content to sit and watch while I treated Magnus for shock with fluids and drugs. Shock itself could be fatal, making him first in line. No broken bones were felt, so while his fluids and drugs were taking effect, I found an appropriate-sized urinary catheter, and back-flushed James's stone into his bladder, releasing a two-day collection of urine down my pant leg. He was relieved in more ways than one, and was a stoic patient for the uncomfortable procedure. After all, he *was* a bulldog. Now we could put him on a special diet to dissolve his stones (if we were lucky) without the need for surgery.

I made my apologies to the folks in the waiting room, and went back to get our three-legged Lab on IV fluids. I had removed his right rear leg a few years back after he made an unsuccessful bid to chew the tire off a UPS truck—while it was driving up the lane. As his fluids continued to drip, I did a quick test for our old and sometimes-fatal nemesis Parvovirus. He was positive.

I called the owner, and had to leave a message. "Patsy, it's Dr. Sharp. Bruce has Parvovirus, and he'll have to stay with us for a while. We'll need to keep him on fluids and supportive care until he's over it, and it may take several days. I know he's had vaccinations, but he missed his appointment last year, and believe it or not, now he's a year overdue. Since he's been vaccinated a lot in the past, his immune system is still going to help, and I think he'll be okay, but it'll be some time before he can come home. I'll check in with you later." She called us back an hour later, surprised, but glad we were able to treat him.

Several days passed. Magnus went home, James could urinate and was gone, and Bruce was getting better. His diarrhea improved, and just when I thought he was going home too, he started to vomit. He vomited every time he ate, and he wasn't doing that when he came in. Strange. Vomiting and diarrhea are common with Parvovirus infections, but they usually occur in the opposite order—vomiting first, then diarrhea, or the two occur simultaneously.

The vomiting went on for two days, with no other signs of illness. Finally I gave him a barium "milkshake"—which is actually a thick, white, vanilla-tasting liquid containing the metal barium. Like any metal, it shows up on X-rays, and allows us to follow the metal milkshake from the stomach, through the intestinal plumbing, all the way to the exit. This would give us a good set of pictures of his G.I. tract on a series of films taken over time—a barium series. Nothing abnormal showed up in the first films of his stomach. Now we would wait about half an hour to see if the stomach had emptied, and the small intestines could be seen.

As I walked Bruce back to his cage, he vomited some barium. Nobody throws up barium. That stuff is as soothing as Pepto-Bismol. If he had just walked in with vomiting as his only sign, what would I think might be wrong? How about a gastric foreign body? Could the barium have concealed a foreign body in his stomach like a spoon in a glass of milk? Parvo might not be the cause of this vomiting at all.

I took another set of X-rays now that his stomach was empty of most of the thick liquid. Then I called the owner.

"You aren't going to believe this! I just took another set of films of Bruce's abdomen after he vomited the barium. There, covered with a thin layer of barium, was the perfect picture of a golf ball, wedged in the first few inches of his intestine."

Patsy said, "You know, I think it was last June, about six months ago, Steve was hitting those plastic practice balls out in the yard and he couldn't find one. I think you just did!"

"Apparently the Parvovirus caused enough turbulence in his stomach and intestine to make the ball leave its harmless place in the stomach, and try to pass down the intestinal tract. It hadn't caused much of a problem until it got stuck. Well, now we know why he's vomiting, but I think you know what's next."

"Surgery?"

"I'll call you when we're done."

Within the next hour I'd retrieved the plastic golf ball, its dimples filled with barium, from its hiding place in the bowel. It now has a place of honor in a drawer in our antique pharmacy cabinet right next to a giant acorn, the hood of a Revell Models 1955 Chevy Bel Air, and the ball I retrieved twice from the stomach of a German Shorthaired pointer. Bruce ate baby food strained chicken and held it down—a good sign. He went home after his week-long ordeal, having survived a virus with potentially fatal consequences, and surgery to fix a dietary indiscretion that showed up six months after a little fun in the backyard. Apparently he thought whacking a ball with a stick was pretty silly compared with chasing it and eating it. It's the closest either of us have ever come to playing golf.

Binx

In the spring there's a part of rural Adams County that seems to bloom more brightly than most. The grass is brighter green, the redbud trees are more pink, and the dogwood slashes stand out on a sunny day like lightning in the trees. The woods aren't empty and cold anymore now that buds are appearing everywhere, and daffodils are popping out all along the tree lines. Flowering trees fill the farms even though the danger of frost may still be there. A longtime resident once said that, "You might even be able to fool someone into thinking this was the Garden of Eden if they were visiting here in April." It was during this beautiful time of the year that a kitten was born, and just as nature had smiled on the fields and woods, so had Binx been blessed. He was exceptional.

I realize that it's hard to find an ugly cat if you study them as individuals. The colors and patterns of cats are unique, and a kitten born in a dark corner of a barn loft may be just as beautiful as one born in a show-cat home. Binx was a tuxedo kitten, shiny jet black with bright white trim. Long-bodied and short-legged, and a Manx by genetics, he was a happy, energetic kitten who loved to play with his littermates. Although Binx now became part of a multiple-cat household on a small farm, he quickly became the family favorite—the signature cat! He stood out from all the other cats and kittens both in appearance and personality.

He was examined at seven weeks, tested negative for feline leukemia, and given his first vaccinations. He was perfectly healthy. He followed the usual course of vaccinations, and grew to be a beautiful cat—sleek mid-length hair, soft, loose skin, long, dramatic white whiskers, purring personality, and just an armload of fun.

In January of that year, when the land was snow-covered, his owner Carol Caldrone made the thirty-minute trip from her farm in Adams County to our office. Young Binx was not acting like himself. He moped around the house, acted tired, and seemed to be losing weight. More alarming yet, at times he just suddenly fell over. When I examined him, he had no fever, but had lost almost half a pound since I had seen him last. He had an elevated heart rate, and he had no Binx-spunk at all.

Now, today, we could have his bloodwork done in our office in twelve minutes, but in 2004 I needed to send it out to a laboratory. We sent it, but I didn't want to wait for the results, so we did an in-office complete blood count manually, and it showed that Binx was anemic. A normal cat has about 35–45 percent red cells in its blood. Binx had only 13 percent.

No wonder he was slow, tired, and felt lousy. He had only about a third of his normal red cells—the oxygen-carrying cells of the blood. This really was an emergency.

Whenever the red cells are low, we consider two things. Is he losing blood somewhere, or not producing enough? He wasn't hemorrhagic, and he wasn't covered with fleas—no loss there. He wasn't bleeding into his intestine, and yet there *was* the possibility of a blood parasite that causes Feline Infectious Anemia, or the autoimmune version of hemolytic anemia. The other major group of problems involves the bone marrow where blood is produced. If he doesn't have enough blood, is he not making it? His white cells in the blood were normal, unaffected, so this was less likely.

Awaiting further lab work, I started him on the treatment for the blood parasite and the immune-mediated problem, thinking this would cause no harm, was easy, and might give him a quick fix should either of these turn out to be the culprit. I also called an internal medicine specialist, and requested an appointment for our special Binx. He could be dying quickly if we didn't find the source of his anemia. Carol took him to Cincinnati for his appointment.

An ultrasound of Binx showed an abdominal mass, and Carol was asked to bring a pair of her other cats to their office to provide blood for a transfusion. The phone call I received from the specialist went something like this: "Rob, I think Binx has one of the rare juvenile malignancies. My plan is to transfuse him, and give him enough of a boost for you to do an exploratory."

The next morning, one of my favorite young cats with one of my favorite cat clients came back from the specialist with what seemed like a no-win situation. I was to do surgery on a dying cat to see why he was dying . . . and if, or when he died, it would be on my surgery table. I didn't like the odds, the responsibility, or the disappointment Carol would feel when I had to tell her that Binx's borrowed time had run out. But Carol deserved a bottom-line diagnosis, and it would now be my job to find it.

Carol kissed him goodbye, handed him to me, and left the office for home. Binx was anesthetized, clipped stem to stern, prepped for surgery, and the instruments were readied. I made the long incision, and immediately ran into an abdomen filled with blood and a tumor. This seven-pound young cat had a mass the size of a hen's egg attached to the left lobe of his liver. The abdomen is a tight squeeze when you want to get a good look at something, and when you add blood and a large mass of cancer, it's difficult to see or feel where the tumor ends and good tissue begins. My solution was to remove that lobe of the liver, and the mass attached to it.

The liver could do without that part anyway, since it had enough left to do its job.

The mass and liver lobe both contained blood, which was lost to Binx when they were removed. The transfusion gave him enough so he could withstand some loss during surgery, but remember, he only weighed seven pounds—not a big guy. I worried that he was still possibly too anemic to survive the stress of surgery. I closed the abdomen, placed him on a blanket in our incubator, set it to a nice warm temperature, let his IV fluids drip slowly, and piped in oxygen. He gradually woke up. I called Carol and told her the situation.

The next morning I called Carol again to let her know that Binx was alive, alert, and actually had some breakfast. We sent the tumor to our pathologist for a definitive diagnosis and waited four days for an answer. Binx was gaining strength in the incubator daily, and by the time the path report was faxed to us, he wanted out.

The lab equivocated between two bad cancers, and wanted to do further tests on the sample to give a final answer. Of course it involved more expense, but Carol gave permission.

Binx was doing well enough to go home and hang out on the couch while we waited for those pathology answers. Carol was surprised when she came to pick him up as he climbed up my lab coat and perched on my shoulder to greet her. It was obvious that he had missed her.

The lab identified the tumor as a hemangiosarcoma, a cancer that frequently metastasized, and said that with chemotherapy our boy might have six to nine more months to live. But we would only be buying time.

When I saw Binx two months later his red cells were back up to 52 percent—great. He was perky at that time, and looked so much better. I was happy that Binx was home, even though his prognosis was bleak. Carol and her favorite tuxedo Manx would have a little more time together.

Carol didn't opt for the chemotherapy, but she worried and fretted and prayed a lot. (She admitted that much of her praying seemed to involve cats. She told me that her diary entry from the day she drove him back to my office from Cincinnati read, "I wanted to share my life with you, Binx, but I guess we'll have to share eternity." She had little hope.)

Even in the spring, when flowers are making the winter seem distant and the woods become so beautiful, there's never a promise that the flowers, or a kitten, will last forever. Binx acted like a normal cat during the six months that he was given to live. And again during the next six months, and the next. In fact, he acted like the healthy cat that we all thought so highly of until his time was up. Binx was buried with all the honors given to a favorite cat in the garden where his grave is marked with an incredible profusion of tulips, daffodils, and hyacinths. Against all odds, he was *seventeen years old* when he died.

There are several things we learned from Binx. I learned that even when the statistics show a bleak forecast, they're only based on numbers and probability. And sometimes they're wrong. I don't doubt Binx's diagnosis, but maybe his surgery put him at a better place on the bell curve of life. I'll never give up hope or treatment now because a number says it's a waste of time.

We watched as Binx lived each day in the present. He never considered the future, and if I told him he had a short time to live, he would walk to his favorite spot where the sunlight made the carpet warm, and take a nap. He never worried, fretted, or cried—at least not in the seventeen years that I knew him. Each day was a good day. "What's this tomorrow you talk about?" Lesson learned.

And as for Carol, she learned that sometimes prayers are answered.

Failure to Communicate

"The single biggest problem with communication is the illusion that it has taken place."

—George Bernard Shaw

Communication

One of the most common problems physicians face when treating humans is compliance. Patients don't do what they're told. These are the same people who don't do what we tell them after we treat their animals.

Maybe they don't understand the reason for the instructions, and add their own touch—like "keeping your dog quiet after surgery" . . . except when you take her out to play. "Give the pills every eight hours" . . . since I'm only awake for sixteen hours a day, that must mean twice a day. Or maybe they didn't tell us something we should know, like putting drops in Harlan's eyes every four hours is impossible since "I'll be at work at the hospital doing twelve-hour shifts."

Larry Spoljaric was a huge cat. He was brought to me as a kitten by a farmer, Casey Spoljaric, who looked exactly like a Midwest farmer in his fifties should look—DeKalb Seed Corn ball cap with the flying wing logo, checkered flannel shirt, bib overalls, and a perpetual tan from the cap on down. He farmed down near Locust Grove, across from the ice cream stand. For the sixteen years that I treated Casey's cat, I never met any other member of his family. He paid by cash, was on time for appointments, and was always compliant with instructions. A good client, and a friendly guy, whenever I saw him in the front of the office, I'd wave and yell, "Hi, Casey!" and he'd wave back with "Hi, Doc."

Larry was dying of kidney disease when he reached old age, and Casey asked that we put him to sleep. I noticed that when he signed the euthanasia permission form he signed his name James Spoljaric. "Is James your proper name and Casey's a nickname?" I asked.

"No, Doc. Casey's my daughter. I put the record in her name since Larry's really her cat. Most people call me Jim."

We had a failure to communicate. *For sixteen years.* I felt pretty dumb.

We're quick to blame clients when they don't follow instructions, but it's possible that the instructions we gave were too vague, or concerned something medical that we easily understood, so we didn't explain the reason for the treatment well enough to the non-medically oriented owner. Maybe we should have talked about it more. We needed to make it foolproof. Every eight hours is really *three times* in a twenty-four-hour day. Quiet means quiet . . . *all day long.* Casey is . . . well, my fault, I guess.

The next stories involve a few examples of well-meaning people doing unexpected things possibly due to a lack of communication.

You Didn't Tell Me . . .

The litter of beagle pups squirmed around on the exam table. The five of them looked like carbon copies, brown, white, and black, stepping on each other's soft, floppy ears. Each had a lump about the size of an English walnut between the shoulder blades. Their owner, Harry Ryan, a cattleman in his fifties who forgot to shave this week, wasn't very pleased.

"Your wormer did this to 'em, Doc. Those bumps are right where I injected 'em and it looks like they're gettin' worse! What should we do? I think we should write a letter to that company and tell 'em about this! That stuff is dangerous!"

I felt the bumps and he was right. "They feel kind of soft and moveable like liquid, but I didn't give you any injectable wormer."

"You sure as hell did!! AnnaMary stopped in Monday afternoon and picked it up!"

I called Missy into the exam room and asked, "Was AnnaMary here Monday, and what did we give her?"—knowing we had no injectable wormers in the office.

"Yes. She stopped in around noon and asked for some wormer for the pups. I thought they weighed around three pounds, so I put three pounds' worth of wormer in each of five syringes and wrapped 'em up in a tissue and charged her for them."

"Mr. Ryan, how did you inject that wormer into these pups? The syringes didn't have any needles on them. That was oral medication."

"I thought it was funny to have a syringe with no needle, so I went to Tractor Supply and bought some. That stuff was pretty thick to go through those needles but I got it done."

"You were supposed to squirt that in their mouths! I don't think it's a big deal, but we'll need to open and drain the abscesses where the wormer was injected."

"I feel pretty stupid, Doc. I wondered why there wasn't needles on those syringes. I guess we won't need that letter."

I made a little incision on each pup, drained the bump, and they all made an uneventful recovery. This isn't the only time that somehow we had assumed the obvious that turned out to be wrong.

"Joanna Quigley's in the large exam room with Midnight. She says he's no better," said Melissa with a funny look.

I walked in, exchanged a few pleasantries with the Methodist choir leader in the chair, all the while petting her cat Midnight, and wondering what the sticky stuff on the bite wound on his back might be. I took his temperature—103.8 F.

"I agree, he doesn't look any better. His wound looks just as angry and his fever is just as high. Has he had his medication?"

"Just like you told me to give it—every twelve hours."

"I know the little eyedroppers in that Amoxicillin liquid can be tricky. Has he had a full dropper each time?"

"Yep, just like you said."

"Does he like the taste?"

"I don't know, I never seen him lick it. I just squirt it on the wound and go about my business."

We have met the enemy and they are us. "Joanna, that Amoxi goes in his mouth, not on the wound. Let's try that instead and I'll recheck him next week."

In a week he was better. I'm sure somehow this misunderstanding was my fault.

Colic in horses can be a terrible thing. The cause can be as simple as an upset stomach from a change of feed, eating some sawdust bedding along with the new hay on the stall floor, or any one of a number of reasons usually cured with some mineral oil and time. It can be as serious as an impacted bowel, a twisted bowel, or a dying piece of intestine requiring immediate surgery or euthanasia. No matter what the cause, the pain can be horrific, causing the horse to throw himself to the ground and roll in pain. A thousand-pound animal rolling uncontrollably can be dangerous both to himself and anyone nearby. As the pain eases, the horse will stand until the next pain when the rolling begins again. This can go on for hours, and is always treated as an emergency.

My home phone rang on a Sunday morning just as I was getting dressed for church. "Dr. Sharp. My name is Joey Frazier and you've never been to our place. My parents are out of town and my sister and I are here alone. Our horse is rolling like something hurts and I don't know what to do. He gets up and walks around a while and then lays down and rolls. Is he sick?"

"I think I better come look at him. Can you give me directions?"

"Do you know where C.T. Dunlap lives? We're the next drive east on Peach Orchard Road."

"It'll take me about a half-hour to get there. Is your horse out on pasture?"

"Yep."

"You get him in, and I'll be right down. Be careful. If he starts to roll, get outta the way!"

I changed my clothes, put on coveralls, checked the truck for a gallon of mineral oil (yes, you'd need that much), and a hand pump and stomach tube to put the oil into the horse. All there. Of course, since it was raining the horse would be wet. Good thing Joey was walking him to the barn. I headed down the Fairfax Pike to the Peach Orchard Road turnoff, the truck's windshield wipers slapping a constant cadence all the way. As I drove up the lane I could see a split-level house, but no barn, or Joey. I was sure I was at the right place because I could see Dunlap's barn up the road.

I went to the front door and knocked. "Is this Fraziers' farm?"

"Yes, and thank God you're here," said the teenage girl at the door. "Joey is with Fury and I think he's really sick."

"Let's go have a look. How do we get to the barn? Should we get in the truck?"

"No, we can walk around back."

We went out the front door and into the rain, and then went around the house. When we approached the home's lower level, Joey met me at the door. "He's in here and seems a little better."

As I walked in, there, between two pairs of bunk beds in a 10'x10' bedroom, stood a dripping black quarter horse wearing a blue tarp. I would guess he'd never been in a house before.

"Holy cow, Joey, when I said get him in, I meant the barn!"

"My parents haven't built one yet."

Immediately we led Fury back outside into the rain. He had a minor upset stomach easily treated with mineral oil. I don't know if Joey ever told his folks that Fury had been in the downstairs bedroom. I don't know what would have happened if he had started to roll in there. But I know that when I say, "Get him in," I now add *the barn*.

Head Games

Randy lived next door. He actually lived outside the house next door. He was a silver and black classic tabby who never passed up an opportunity to place his head where it could receive the most petting. Because he was an outside cat, he wandered the neighborhood, and we played with him in our yard too. That's the good news, but because he was an outside cat his life expectancy was about half what it would be if he stayed inside his home. That's not just a guess; those are statistical facts.

His owners were friendly people with two kids, a boy, Terry, and a girl named Amy. Since we had an Amy, it was hard to refer to one or the other without a final letter—B or S. So Amy S. played with Amy B. for years, and Randy played with both. The girls dressed him up, put him on the swing, carried him around, and generally treated him like a third member of the Walnut Street Gang. I supposed you could say that Randy loved them. He purred even while he was being carried like a bagpipe, and would run to whichever girl came out of either house to see what their next adventure would be. He was never put off by their games of "hide the cat."

Amy B.'s dad called me one evening when I had just finished dinner and said, "Rob, can I give a cat an aspirin?"

"I wouldn't, but why do you ask?"

"Well, I can bring him in tomorrow. What time will you open?"

"Why? What's wrong?"

"I think I may have grazed Randy when I parked the van tonight. He looks okay, but he's probably just sore. His eyes are kinda red around the edges."

"That's it! Red around the edges is the clincher. Put him in the van and meet me at the office, Jim. I'll see him right now." I once had a client describe his dog's eye as "pretty red all around" and when I talked him out of using the "Visine Fix" that he wanted to perform, and he brought Fred to the office, I found an eye out of the orbit and drying fast. I always insist on seeing an eye—no pun here.

Well, Randy's eyes *were* red around the edges all right. *Both* eyes were out of their orbits and the lids were behind the eyes. One eye out of its "socket" is uncommon, and a double is unheard of. And no one had noticed that Randy's jaw was broken in several places. A faint tire mark was visible on top of his head. Randy's head had been driven over. Without treatment, if he had lived, by morning his eyes would have been dry and useless since blinking was impossible. He was shocky, with white gums and a racing heart rate. Randy was in serious trouble. Aspirin wasn't the answer.

I explained what I saw and said, "Just leave him with me, Jim. We've got to deal with shock and get his eyes treated tonight. If he's up to it, I'll wire his jaw tomorrow. I'll need some X-rays to see if anything else is injured, but there's no reason for you to stick around now. This is going to take a while. I'll treat him like he's mine, Jim, after all, he's both Amys' favorite cat, and mine too."

I started IV fluids and drugs, and treated Randy for shock. I kept his eyes from drying out with constant applications of drops. After an hour or so he was stable enough that I could anesthetize him and repair his "bilateral traumatic proptosis" as the description in his record would call it. When he woke up at least I only had his broken jaw to repair. Just replacing his eyes was a major step forward and time-sensitive. I spent most of the next morning taking several X-ray views of Randy, making sure he had no skull fracture, and then wiring his mandibular fractures back together. It wasn't perfect, since a couple of teeth had been left on the road. He spent several days at the office learning to eat baby food, which he loved, and was sent home to Amy B. with frequent visits by Amy S. Cats are great healers, and there's a saying that probably originated in the days of the first orthopedist, that if you put the two ends of a cat's fracture together in the same room, they'll heal. With dogs, careful alignment of broken parts is more critical. Randy healed, and after a couple of months I removed the wire and pins from his mouth, and he was back to his purring self, crunching dry food.

When it rains an outside cat has to be creative if he wants to stay comfortable. You won't see a cat sitting in the yard getting soaked. Maybe a dog would do this, but a cat has more sense about these things. It was pouring, and Randy found a great place to stay dry under Jim's conversion van parked in front of the house. It never occurred to him that sleeping with your head under the front of a tire was a bad thing—after all, it wasn't moving. Another example of why an outside cat has half the life expectancy of his indoor sibling.

Jim got up in the morning, showered, got dressed, had breakfast, hurried out to his van since it was raining, and left for work. The bump he felt was Randy's head.

"I can't believe this happened again," he said as he carried Randy into the office. "He probably isn't hurt. His eyes look fine but I thought you should take a look, Rob."

"Well, his eyes look fine, but his jaw is broken again. Go on to work and we'll take care of Randy." I wired his jaw and teeth back in place, being careful to place both ends of each fracture together as closely as I could. After all, he had some irregular areas left over from last time.

Jim picked him up after work, and I gave him the talk about "only so many times . . . he's going to be killed . . . why don't you . . . fourteen years of life vs. seven years"—all the things that sounded reasonable to *me* anyway.

Not everything goes the way you'd like it. Randy healed like a good cat would, and played in the yard with the girls, but he was still an outside cat.

A short time later, Randy and his family moved away, and we only kept in touch through their relatives in Hillsboro. But no one knew anything about Randy, whose head had been driven over twice. I'd like to think he lived out his life in the warm Florida sun, on a beach far away from car tires, or maybe even as an indoor cat lounging in air conditioning. Amy B. became a professional and has kids of her own now. Amy S. works with animals and people every day, helping to make their lives better, and her cats (and there have been a quite a few) live in the house—of course.

Cleaned!

"Do it yourself" isn't something farmers believe in, it's something they do, and something they've done since the first crop was put in the ground. When a settler's plow snapped do you think he called the John Deere dealership to send out a repairman? Those self-reliant genes and skills have been passed down through generations, so a country kid thinks he can fix anything, do anything, and will call for help only in a real pinch. Most farms have a workshop filled with tools, welding equipment, and spare parts for about everything, and the kids have taken classes in school in agricultural mechanics and homemaking. City kids have rarely been up close to a combine, let alone welded the grain head when it cracked.

So it isn't unusual for this same attitude to be carried over into livestock. A vet gets called if the farmer and his neighbors can't diagnose and fix the sick critter. When a calf is trying to be born, the farmer will, and rightly so, try to help the cow himself. Sometimes speed matters. When he can't do it, he might get his family or a neighbor to help. "Pulling" a stuck calf might require some finesse and some manipulation of the seventy-five-pound baby, but brute strength is usually tried first. And second, third, and so on. . . . The vet is called when all else has failed. When I arrived at some farms, I felt the hood of the tractor to make sure it wasn't warm from an attempted obstetrical delivery!

Bill Newkirk was a good farmer, scientific in his crop techniques, and up to date when it came to herd practices with his dairy cattle. He was usually the exception to the do-it-yourself practice. Whenever he had a cow with an illness, he would call for professional help, and just before Christmas, he called the office.

"Hi, Melissa! This is Bill Newkirk. How's everything?"

"Hangin' in there, stranger. How's everything in Tranquility?"

"Well, it could be better. I have a heifer that didn't clean. Can Doc come take a look at her sometime today?"

Now "cleaning" a cow is a little controversial. After a cow has delivered her calf, she usually passes the membranes that surrounded it—the placenta—in a fairly short time. This is a pretty large piece of tissue—big enough to enclose a seventy-five-pound calf. When she doesn't pass it, a certain percentage, which is usually way more than the farmer wants to see, hangs down behind her, sometimes most of the way to the ground. Old-timers might tie a sock filled with rocks to this mess in the hope that this added weight would pull it out. Brave farmers might put on a glove or plastic sleeve of some sort and pull, only to have it stretch and snap off about two feet from their hand. Authorities taught that it should be left alone. It would separate from the uterus eventually and drop out. Good in theory, but there's a problem—after a few days it became so odiferous that every time the cow came into the parlor to be milked, the folks in there couldn't stand it. And so a vet is called—modern theories notwithstanding. What might be good for the cow was bad for the farmer.

The technique for "cleaning" a cow is simple. The big girl is brought into the milking parlor and while she's pinched between the rails to prevent dancing around, the vet can go to work dislodging the dangling afterbirth from the uterus.

"I'll give Doc a call on the radio, Bill. He's over at the Simpsons' farm right now, but he can swing by on his way back to town."

As I pulled into Bill's farm I was always impressed by the orderliness of the place. The lawn was always cut in perfect stripes. The tall white barn could be on the cover of *County Living* magazine, with blue-flowered curtains in the windows and a perfect white gravel drive leading up to the main doors. The family farmhouse matched the barn, and was also white with blue shutters. White board fencing stretched as far as you could see, down the pasture behind the barn. This was a "Century Farm," so designated because a member of this same family had been the owner for at least a hundred years.

"Hey, Bill, good to see ya!"

"I've already got her in the parlor, Doc. She's a little wild since she's a first-calf heifer. She calved last week but hasn't cleaned yet. She's gettin' pretty ripe."

The patient stood quietly chewing some grain Bill had dropped into the milking stall feed pan. Usually four cows are milked, diagonally next to each other with four more on the opposite side of the "pit" where the milkers work. This herringbone pattern is where the parlor design got its name. Each cow has her favorite spot and amazingly, will file into the parlor from the outside lot in the same order each milking. They like it here. They're fed some grain and are relieved of the uncomfortable swelling in their udder. They like it even better if you play music!

I put a latex glove on my left hand followed by another glove called a plastic "sleeve" that reached to my shoulder. Double-gloving prevented a possible breakthrough. Most veterinarians palpate cows and do procedures like this with their left hand. It leaves the right hand free to write in the herd record, and if something goes poorly while your arm is in there, such as a violent move by a thousand-pound Holstein, it prevents your dominant arm from being broken. Also it seems like you ought to be able to train your left hand to do something if you're a "righty." So in went my left hand and arm for the treasure hunt.

"I think this is only attached in a couple of places, Bill. We should be done in a few minutes."

The placenta of a cow is attached to the uterus in a pattern of contact places each about the size of a lemon. The reason why the experts want this to be left alone is because forced removal can damage the uterus or leave some tissue behind. I was careful detaching the recalcitrant afterbirth, and as it dropped to the parlor floor, we were half done. I always deposited four antiseptic uterine boluses, a kind of pill each about the size of your index finger but four times as thick, into the uterus while my sleeve was still on to help deal with any infection. Then I gave her a couple of injections and pronounced her "cleaned."

Bill thanked me and I was on my way. Over the years I repeated this same procedure at the Newkirk farm at least a dozen times, and before me, Dr. Lukhart had probably done the same. The Newkirks had close to a hundred dairy cows and each had a calf every year. Cleaning wasn't a common procedure, but it wasn't rare either. It was a job most dairymen would rather leave to someone else—me.

One February, while I was in another part of the state visiting my parents, Bill Newkirk stopped in the office. "Hey, Missy. I know Doc's going to be gone for a little while. I have a cow that didn't clean and I wondered if he'd mind if I did it myself?"

"I'll call him on the phone and you can ask him."

"Doc, I've got a cow that freshened a week ago and didn't clean. I wondered if I can have the stuff you give cows after you clean 'em and a sleeve. I'm afraid to wait till you get back and I've watched you do this a hundred times. I know I can do it."

"Sure, Bill. Give both injections in the muscle when you're done, and four uterine boluses. Put Missy back on and I'll tell her what to give you."

"Thanks, Doc. You know I'd have you out if you were in town."

Two weeks passed. I was back in the office seeing Stella the Scottie for a limp when Bill Newkirk came in the office with his left arm in a cast.

"Geez, Bill, what happened?"

"You won't believe it, Doc. I cleaned that ol' cow just fine. All that smelly afterbirth came droppin' right outta there, but as I was finishing I had a little trouble. I gave her the shots right where you told me. I got my balling gun and went around to the front to give her those pills. I got her in a headlock and was about to jam one in her mouth when she shook that big head of hers and whacked my elbow into the parlor rail. If that was how she was going to act I figured she'd have to do without those pills, and I went straight to the emergency room. This cast will be on for six more weeks. Want to sign it?"

"Be glad to. You know why I didn't have that trouble when I did it?"

He gave me a puzzled look.

"I put the uterine boluses in the other end of the cow!"

"Now You Tell Me This . . ."

Anna Marie Tricomi was a grouch. There's just no other way to say it. Well, maybe there is . . . she was crabby, demanding, sullen, paranoid, unsatisfiable . . . she had it all. And unfortunately, she was my client. But she had a really nice cat—Bubbles.

I had been Mrs. Tricomi's veterinarian since I came to Hillsboro, probably because she'd been thrown out of every other vet's office, and I was the new guy. I tried to be as nice to her as I was to anyone else. Some people don't make it easy, though, and when she was in the exam room with Bubbles I tried to concentrate on the problem at hand. Any stray conversation would launch her into a tirade about some perceived wrong that had befallen her and the incompetent idiot who was responsible. Gas prices, snowfall, runny fried eggs, sermons, Republicans, child-rearing, Democrats, and human behavior in general were all subjects of potential rants and taboo areas to even brush near with a stray word. I was very careful to talk primarily to Bubbles and only ask about signs of the current problem. I knew that probably I was the incompetent idiot when Mrs. Tricomi was in other locales, and so I didn't want to give her any more cannon fodder than necessary.

Bubbles and I were friends. It is a testament to the great ability of a cat to ignore and rise above the human failings they are subjected to by their owners. They know they're superior animals (just ask one) and choose to ignore what they wish. This is the only reason that Mrs. Tricomi had a pet that hadn't run off for good. Bubbles ignored her.

Mrs. Tricomi had a unique way of starting a conversation. She would scowl at me and out would come the dreaded, "Now you tell me this . . ." Not in a pleasant, questioning way, but more like the way a mother would begin a conversation with a teenager who came home with a nose ring. It would be followed by the current complaint. For example, "Now you tell me this—why does this cat drink so much water with his supper when he knows that he will just have to wake me up going to his litter pan in the middle of the night? Can't you fix this?" Or, "Now you tell me this—why, after all the money I've spent on flea products at this place, does this cat still go outside and play with that filthy fleabag Fredrick, the McMurrays' cat?"

How do you answer questions like that? Obviously you can't, and thereby become another incompetent idiot on her long list. I knew that, and accepted it, because Bubbles and I were friends. He was a purring delight, fat and cuddly, rolling on the exam table with the enthusiasm of a cat that was only petted once a year and this was it.

In forty years of practice I have only told two people that I wanted them to start seeing another veterinarian—essentially giving them the "bum's rush"—and Mrs. Tricomi was one of them. It happened on a day in July when I was packed tightly with appointments and running about forty-five minutes behind. I was being interrogated about some medication that I had sent home with Bubbles six months earlier when he had had a bladder infection. Mrs. T. had called Ohio State University's College of Veterinary Medicine to ask what urinary acidifier was currently in use. They could have given at least ten good answers, but of course the one selected didn't match the one I used. (Keep in mind, Bubbles was cured using the stuff I sent home.) And so I was now in the inquisition, facing "Now you tell me this . . ." for about the sixth straight question, when I couldn't take it anymore.

"Mrs. Tricomi, if the way I treat Bubbles doesn't meet with your approval, then I want you to take him to another veterinarian. I won't see him anymore! *This is IT!*"

Her answer to what would have been an insult to a lesser grouch was, "I would never consider that. I enjoy these discussions so! Now you tell me this . . ." I couldn't even throw her out. We were apparently bonded like the Ancient Mariner and his albatross.

A stray cat had begun to hang out around Mrs. Tricomi's house. She was a calico, had a green nasal discharge, was thin, and uncatchable. Mrs. T. felt, since I dealt with animals, that it was my responsibility to catch this cat and get rid of it. It was, after all, a health threat to Bubbles and therefore in my area of responsibility. After four months of complaints about the stray's presence, the cat finally disappeared, and now the problem became her absence. Daily phone calls to the shelter inquiring about "her lost cat" were made. Ads were placed in the paper. It really bothered Mrs. Tricomi that her stray might have met with foul play. She had heard of "cults" that stole cats to do unmentionable things to their "private parts." (Paranoia was in the mix of her attributes.)

One day Melissa came into the exam room and interrupted my examination of a collie with diarrhea. "Dr. Sharp, Mrs. T's here with her cat that's been hit by a car!" I immediately thought Bubbles had been hit crossing Willow Street and I went directly to the treatment room.

There, on the table, was a burlap sack and a crying Mrs. Tricomi. "Let's have a look at him, Mrs. Tricomi. Maybe it isn't that bad."

I opened the bag carefully, but wasn't prepared for what I saw. The body of a black cat, flat as a pancake, dead for *weeks*, was in the bag. Neither Bubbles nor the calico stray, but a random road kill. What exactly did she want me to do with this flat cat?

"Do you know this cat, Mrs. Tricomi?" I asked, trying to correlate the tears with the bag.

"That's what I want you to tell me, Sharp. Is this my lost cat?"

Easy answer. "No. Your stray cat was a calico. Three colors and female. This is a black male. This is not your cat."

"Now you tell me this . . ." (here it comes) "if this cat was in the street for a couple of weeks being driven over by car after car, wouldn't he get black from the dirt? Isn't this my cat?" Sob, sob.

"No, Mrs. Tricomi. This cat's a male. Your cat was a female. The cars couldn't change that."

"What a relief! Please dispose of this cat as you see fit," she said as she wheeled around and headed out the door to the parking lot. I was left literally holding the bag.

These incidents set the stage for a medical event that happens so rarely that many veterinarians have never seen it occur. Good thing too, since it's one of the worst things that can happen to an animal—an anaphylactic reaction.

Allergic reactions to vaccinations are not common. They usually take the form of hives, itching, or swelling at the injection site. All are treatable with a little Benadryl or cortisone. No big deal. But an anaphylactic reaction is sudden, and frequently fatal. Breathing stops and an animal collapses. An acute, violent attack caused by the immune system in revolt. Immediate epinephrine is the only treatment.

Bubbles was on the exam table for his yearly physical and immunizations. He was ten years old and in good health. Mrs. Tricomi was on a rant about the immorality of politicians. I gave Bubbles an injection I'd given many times before, but this time the result was frightening. He collapsed in a few seconds and was not breathing. An anaphylactic reaction! And the cat of the Grand Inquisitor herself. Could this get worse?

I ran to the treatment area with Bubbles in hand, placed him on the sink, clipped the hair off his neck, and put epinephrine directly into his jugular vein. I gave Dopram as a respiratory stimulant and started an IV line. Bubbles breathed. Not dead yet. Mrs. Tricomi was back in the exam room, tissue in hand, sobbing. Bubbles breathed again. Treatment continued.

Through sheer luck and the grace of God, Bubbles survived, and I gladly faced the inquisition that followed. "Now you tell me this . . ."

Time passed and Mrs. Tricomi became too old to live alone. Her son came from somewhere in the East to take her and Bubbles to live with him. Before leaving, she asked her son to take her to my office for a few final matters she wanted to discuss with me. Melissa made the appointment.

Walking with a cane, bent over and frail, she asked to be put in a private room. I walked into the exam room expecting another final round of complaints about something, when an amazing and totally unexpected thing happened. Mrs. Tricomi walked over to my side of the table, placed her cane over her arm, and hugged me.

Now *you* tell me this . . .

Bad Situations

"What happens if you get scared half to death twice?"

—Steven Wright

Bad Situations

After graduating from Miami University, I stayed on as a graduate teaching assistant while I worked on a master's degree in zoology. In the summer I taught the laboratory portion of general zoology that accompanied the lecture given by a professor. When we came to the discussion of reptiles, I went downstairs to the herpetology lab and brought up eight terrariums, each with a different non-poisonous snake. They normally lived in these enclosures, which were built to be mobile for teaching purposes.

The morning lab of twenty students went well. I talked about the amazing skin surface of snakes, and their beautiful patterns of color. We discussed the fact that snakes were very smooth and not slimy at all, and talked about their remarkable ability to climb a tree having no arms or legs. Snakes were our friends, performing rodent control, bug control, and all the other things the textbooks talked about. All went well. The students were fascinated.

The lab class after lunch was a little larger, and listened closely as I followed the book extolling the virtues of these creatures. But just before class started I noticed that the banded water snake was missing from his terrarium. He'd snuck out by lifting the lid of his enclosure, and now was loose in the room. I didn't mention this until I had talked about the non-slimy beneficial snake, and hit the part about "each of you would probably like to hold one" pretty hard. "There is nothing about a snake to be disliked."

Although I said all that, I personally didn't believe a word of it. I thought snakes were slithering, creepy, unpredictable buggers that were fine as long as their space and mine never intersected. Any jokes involving a hoe or a shotgun, while unfounded and crude, were told by people with my view of these legless varmints. They gave me both the willies and the heebie-jeebies.

I finished the lecture with, "By the way, there's a banded water snake loose in the room. If he's near your seat, would you gently pick him up and bring him home to his terrarium?"

What followed was screaming and general confusion. Girls jumped on tables, football players headed for the door, and generally a group of twenty-five college students demonstrated that they held snakes in the same high regard that I did.

As the teacher, I was placed in the position of finding and grabbing the three-foot escapee myself (a job I dreaded), or else appearing as though the lecture I had just given was 100 percent baloney. This part was not in the textbook, but the snake didn't read the book or follow the rules. He didn't know he wasn't allowed out of his terrarium. Animals are never as agreeable or predictable as we'd like. As for the students, they did react predictably—like most nineteen-year-olds would when told there might be a snake under their seat.

The next group of stories involves other animals who created bad situations for a veterinarian, and in some cases even dangerous ones.

In the end, I found the snake under a radiator, held my breath, grabbed his front end while the rest wrapped around my arm, and carried him back to his terrarium. Class dismissed.

Billy

Joni Smyth was raised on a farm. It didn't bother her to put on coveralls, feed the cattle, drive a tractor, or do any of those other things that most people think of as a man's job. One day I was driving down the Marshall Pike, and coming toward me was a gigantic combine taking up most of the road. The driver was waving like crazy, and I thought something was wrong. It was just Joni saying hi. She could see my vet truck from quite a distance from her perch up in the cab. She was just as experienced as her husband Tom on most equipment, and when he was out of town on business, the work of running the grain/cattle operation was done without a hitch.

She called late one night, when most of these calls seem to happen. "Rob, I was out in the field checking on the cows and one of 'em is down. I think she's tryin' to calve. I looked up the records on Number 306 and she should be due any time. Would you mind very much comin' out and checkin' her?"

I'd been to the farm quite a few times and knew the way. Her beef cattle were mostly Angus crosses and mostly black. On a dark night in an unlit field they might be hard to see. Only a good cattle farmer would notice a problem.

"We can load your stuff on the tractor, Rob. It's probably better than takin' your truck. The ground is soft from the rain, and I'd feel better getting the old 4020 covered with mud. The cow's way out near the middle of the field."

"If we have to pull the calf we'll need a lot of gear. Is there room?"

"We have a big box on the back that Tom uses for tools. Most of that stuff should fit."

We loaded all the drugs and gloves into a stainless-steel bucket. The calf puller and hardware were loaded into the toolbox. We went through the gate and started across the field with Joni driving and me perched on the fender. We bounced our way in the dark using the John Deere's headlights to find the cow. It was a moonless night and very dark but we found her, and she was in fact down and wouldn't get up. I put on a sleeve, lubed it up, and went around the back of the cow to check things out. Since she was lying down, I'd have to lie down in the grass to be able to get my arm in with the calf.

"She's got a calf stuck, Joni, and I can feel the front legs but its head is turned back. I may be able to turn the head if I can reach in far enough. Can you hand me those chains and some lube?"

"The lube's right here, but I think the chains are back on your tailgate. I think I saw them as we pulled out—I'll go back and get 'em."

"Thanks, she's being really good. I'll keep trying to sort things out in here while you're gone."

"Be right back, Rob!" and with that she chugged off into the darkness back toward the truck. She took our light source with her, as her headlights found the way to where I'd parked. The stars and the Milky Way overhead made this problem seem very small.

My problem was more one of feeling than seeing anyway. My arm was being squeezed by contractions, and I could barely reach the nostrils of the calf's head, which was obviously facing north while the rest of the calf was headed south. I'd have to pull it around, which isn't that uncommon but still an obstetrical challenge. I needed those chains. I relaxed for a minute and rolled from my left side onto my back with my arm still in the cow. I could hear Joni coming in the distance.

Since it was spooky dark, and I was feeling my way around the unborn calf, my eyes had been shut. I felt something drip on my face and I opened my eyes. Above me only inches away I could see a large ring, a huge wet nose, and the most close-up view of a bull I'd ever had. Somehow in the quiet, this large Charolais bull had gradually eased up to see what was going on.

"Get back, Billy! Get back, Billy!" I could hear Joni yell in the background. The tractor was approaching. "Get back, back, back!"

Billy pulled his face out of my ear and raised his head. I was motionless.

Joni came around the front of the bull and yelled, "Back up, back up!"

He didn't move. So Joni went to the box in the tractor and got a three-foot-long wooden pole. She came around front and smacked this twenty-five-hundred-pound giant right on the nose. No one was more surprised than Billy. He backed straight up, like a locomotive in reverse, and stopped, facing us from about thirty yards away. He pawed the ground but held his spot.

"Sorry, Rob, I forgot he was in this field. He probably wouldn't hurt you—just curious. I'll stay here and keep him away while you work. He's afraid of this stick."

Imagine—a bull weighing well over a ton afraid of a woman with a stick! He sure was!! He never moved. He snorted like his nose hurt. He stood like a huge white ghost in the dark but never approached again. Even though he could demolish a building as easily as a Kenworth tractor-trailer hitting a stop sign, he wasn't going to try his luck with Joni and her stick.

After what seemed like forever, I delivered the calf, and the mother got up and began to help her baby nurse. We loaded my equipment on the old tractor and made our way back to my truck. Joni drove, and I kept an eye out behind us for Billy. He wasn't going to sneak up on me again.

Horseplay

Gelding horses was quite a job back in the days when everyone relied on them for transportation and farm work. Veterinarians did some of the surgery, but laymen did a lot too. Farmhands, blacksmiths, farriers, and local intellectuals would all try their hand at it. After all, they thought, you only needed a stallion, about six or more strong men, a kitchen knife, and a mile of rope. Most thousand-pound stallions didn't give up their testicles that easily, and the days of modern anesthetics were quite a way off in the future. The procedure was dangerous, both to the horse and the men, and nowadays we'd say it was barbaric.

With modern anesthetics, it became safer and more pain-free for both the stallion and the surgeon. It really didn't require a team of men, but could still be dangerous if the plan went south. A lot of horse owners are teenage girls with parents who agreed to let their daughter take a horse in 4-H. They know nothing about horses and neither does the kid. Some horse owners think the call to the vet is the last responsibility they have, and when appointment time arrives, they show you the horse and then go inside to watch *Wheel of Fortune*. A veterinarian has to learn to do this procedure alone, because from a safety standpoint, having an onlooker nearby might be dangerous anyway. It still becomes necessary to get a large animal both onto the ground, and then back up again safely. Sounds easy? Think about getting a two-hundred-fifty-pound drunk stranger in a local bar, who doesn't speak English, to stop acting like a jerk and lie down without swinging body parts in your direction or falling on you. Then imagine that he weighs a thousand pounds, and try it using only a rope to help you. Some skill is involved but luck's always welcome.

The Browns bought their kid a pony. I never met their youngster since he or she was in school at the time I went to their "farm." I never saw the Browns because they were at work until late at night. They had made arrangements over the phone to have me geld their pony while no one was home, which is something I can't believe now I had agreed to do. Surely someone else made this appointment.

It sounded simple. The pony was always tied to a tree during the day, and would give me "no trouble at all." He was gentle, and a "real sweetheart" to be around. When I was done I could tie him to the same tree and he would be happy to stand and eat grass until they got home. "He's our baby, and we wouldn't want anything to happen to him. We heard from the horse club that you're the best."

The Browns' house was only about a half-mile down the road from the office. To put it another way, the Browns lived on US Route 50, the busy east-west state route that went straight through Hillsboro on its way between Cincinnati and Chillicothe. On the day of the appointment I left the office and was there in less than five minutes. There, tied to a maple tree in the front yard, was a fat black and white Shetland pony—the patient.

I walked up to him, talked with him a little, and when we were done I thought he was indeed a friendly guy. For the sake of the anesthetic I guessed him to be around 500 pounds, or about half a horse. He apparently lived in the garage and back field because there wasn't any barn to be seen, and I hoped he had a better life than just being tied to a tree.

I got out all the instruments, drugs, syringes, bucket, soap and water, and other stuff that I'd need. I left his own twenty-five-foot rope tied to the tree since it would keep him in his area, and attached my rope to his halter that I'd need to help him down to the ground and back up. I gave the first part of his anesthetic in the jugular vein, and as predicted, he quickly lowered his head and stood motionless. After a couple of minutes I gave the second drug. This one completes the process and *most* horses lie down quickly. The goal is to keep the pony's head from smacking the ground.

Having not read the manual, the pony stood up on his hind legs after the second injection and started to go in reverse. He backed up, drugged and wild-eyed, and when he reached the end of his rope, it snapped. The old rope was no match for his frantic 500 pounds. I still held a rope attached to his halter that I was going to use to guide his head to the ground, but it wasn't tied to anything. You'd think having a semi-conscious horse careening around was bad enough, but as he continued to back up I realized—my God, he's headed toward Route 50! I dug my feet in and pulled on the head rope. I couldn't stop him. He still weighed a whole lot more than I did, and I could only barely affect his wobbling path. As the drugs took over, he slowed down and began to fall. I pulled on the head rope and when he finally went down—gracefully, I might add—he was sleeping in the ditch on the edge of the road that runs from Ocean City, Maryland, to Sacramento, California. Cars drove by constantly with gawkers undoubtedly wondering what was going on. "Some nut's down in the ditch with a horse!" "The horse must have been hit!" I pressed on with my surgery as if I were in the middle of an eighty-acre field. My head was really close to the road at times. I didn't look up, I protected my incision when eighteen-wheelers blew by, and I moved as fast as I could, knowing that these drugs wouldn't last forever and pretty soon Ronnie the pony would be getting up.

My lariat was much stronger than the pony's rope, so I tied it through the ring in his halter, drove my truck up on the front lawn grass in line with the maple tree, tied the other end of the rope to my Reese hitch, and waited. He couldn't go onto the road now. It's not good to have a pony get up before he's ready, so I put my ball cap over his "up" eye for shade, knelt lightly on his neck, and passed the time while he slowly came around. When I thought he was ready I helped him up, and there he stood. We conversed for a while.

When he could walk toward his tree, I led him. If he took off, he would only get as far as my truck would allow since he was tied to the hitch. When he was near the maple, I untied the rope from my truck and tied him to his tree—just like I found him.

He wasn't killed on US 50. He didn't cause an accident. He was gelded as requested. That evening his owner got home and called my house. "Ronald looks real good. He's eating and there's hardly any swelling. Thanks a lot, Doc. By the way, I noticed he has a different rope on him. It looks like a lariat. Did you need to use that for some reason?"

Minnis

Minnis Monroe lived and died like a man on a model train layout. Frozen in time, his era would surely have been set back in the fifties with steam engines circling the village, and like the things on that trainboard, nothing ever changed for him. His farm equipment was at least forty years old and covered with a coating of rust. His house was painted so long ago that now the boards were just grey wood, and you couldn't guess the original color. On top flapped a rusted metal roof. His animals belonged to breeds that no local farms raised, and his farming practices were techniques that modern farmers left behind when one-row corn pickers and a horse-drawn sleigh ride to church were common. He had lived with his mother all his life and when she died, he never changed a thing. He was born in that house and there he lived his life. He was stuck in the fifties and happier days.

The Monroe farm was deep in that part of the county where no ground is really flat and no roads are straight. You couldn't see his place from the blacktop and the turnoff was a dirt lane bordered by weeds. It would be a great place to hide from all those worries that make people hide out. There hid Minnis, alone and trying to stay in a lost period, waiting for something that would never come back.

He raised Poland China hogs, Shorthorn cattle of the beef variety, chickens, and planted corn and soybeans on the back eighty acres using equipment his grandfather used when an eighty-acre field was a big farm. He was a longtime client of Dr. Lukhart and as a result, became a client of mine. In spite of his backward ways, he was a likable man, kind to his animals, and content with his life on the farm.

He drove his old Ford truck to town one fall day and stuck his head in the office door. "Is Doc available some day this week, Melissa? I've got some baby pigs that I'd like him to cut. Any day this week is okay."

"He can come out Friday morning if that's good for you."

"That's fine. Can he come early? You know cuttin' pigs is stressful on 'em and I'd like to get it done before the heat of the day."

"How early are we talkin' about here, Minnis? We open at eight-thirty and he could be there by nine. First appointment, is that all right?"

"Oh, no. I'd like him at the farm by six. I'll have 'em penned up and separated from the sows by then. See if that works for him."

She came back to my office and asked, and I answered, "Six o'clock in the morning? Is he kidding? When does he think I work? Tell him I'll be there by seven, no sooner. I'll have to get up and be on the road by six-thirty, even so. Aww, man, why am I agreeing to this?"

"I'll tell him" was all she said. I'm sure she cleaned it up a little.

Friday came, and I was on the road by six-thirty. I was working for myself then, and could set my own hours. Just like now. Driving in the morning twilight down an obscure road to castrate eighty pigs at the literal crack of dawn. I should have my head examined.

I bounced up the dirt lane toward the collapsing bank barn, and there was Minnis, waiting for me with a pen of twenty-pound pigs. "I thought you got lost. We've been waitin' for you about a half-hour." This must have been the "royal" we, or else he meant that he and the pigs were waiting, since there wasn't anyone else there to help.

"Cutting pigs" is a relatively simple surgery as castrations go. It's a two-person job, a catcher and a "surgeon." Some farmers do it without a veterinarian since it doesn't take a lot of surgical skill. The catcher grabs a pig by the hind legs and lifts him up, swinging his head and back between his legs to hold him, with the pig's stomach facing out so the surgeon can have access to the area of interest. The pigs do try to bite when they're being held, so a good knee-squeeze is critical.

Two quick small cuts are made, and two "oysters" are exteriorized and removed. The pig is marked with a big orange crayon and put back on the ground—done. The problem is that lifting a twenty-pound pig isn't hard for most folks, but lifting and holding eighty pigs that size will wear you out. Most farmers have help taking turns lifting, but not Minnis. About the time we finished pig number 40, an episode occurred that still gives me the willies as I tell you about it.

Poland China hogs are a breed that was first developed in Ohio, in fact about eighty miles from where we were standing. The largest hog ever recorded was a Poland China weighing 2,552 pounds, which is heavier than a Holstein bull standing six feet tall. A full-grown sow might weigh seven hundred pounds up to a half-ton, and can move with surprising speed for such a large critter. Arnold Ziffel on *Green Acres* was really just a baby. If allowed to grow to maturity, he would have been a really big boy.

What do you think is missing when I say we had a pen of eighty baby pigs? Their mothers, and like most moms they aren't happy when someone takes their babies away and makes them cry. Squealing offspring upset and infuriated these worried sows.

The separated big girls were being held in a pen about thirty yards from where we were working. They were in an enclosure built and maintained with the same care and maintenance as the rest of the farm, and now they were starting to make some sounds. Their loud, deep oinks were mixed with the sound of wood cracking and splintering and lots of breathing noises. A dozen mad sows were breaking out.

These angry mothers had some factors in their favor. There were a dozen of them and two of us. They were each four or five times bigger than we were. They weren't dumb, and they weren't happy. And now they were coming after us—a stampede of enraged swine looking for the guys who hurt their babies.

"Head for the barn, Doc. The sows are loose!"

I didn't know how long it would take for them to close the gap between their former enclosure and our chicken-wire pigpen, but I could guess what kind of protection that flimsy wire would be against a pack of peeved porkers. I jumped the chicken wire and followed Minnis to the barn as fast as my rubber-booted feet could run. Minnis was waiting in the doorway with a 2 × 4 in his hands, holding it like a baseball bat.

"Climb the ladder! Fast!" he said to me. With a swing like a designated hitter in a close game, Minnis whipped that board around and hit the first sow that came through the doorway. It not only didn't stop her, it didn't even slow her down. He jumped to the side like a matador and landed on a cornpicker that gave him a little shelter. *Olé!* The sows had their mouths open with huge teeth showing. Bellowing noises and drool were all I noticed as I watched from my perch on the decayed ladder going to the haymow. I'd read an account of a farmer gone missing, only later identified by some hair and dentures found in the enclosure with the hogs. Those pigs weren't even mad. I didn't have dentures to aid in my identification so I was staying put on the ladder.

Some of the sows stopped outside the barn near their little ones, and some rushed into the barn looking for the pignappers. Eventually, they settled down, the squealing stopped, and everyone was calm again. I came down from the antique ladder and we plotted our course forward.

"That was a close one, Doc!" was all Minnis said. Nothing more would be done that day.

We tried again at seven o'clock the following Friday and finished the rest of the pigs. This time the sows were locked in the barn. Other than being too late in the day for Minnis, it went well. And it went well for the years that followed.

Every fall, his corn was put into standing shocks. He had no combine, so harvest took until the snow fell. In the spring he planted with the planter his grandfather used, a couple rows at a time, which took until summer. His herd of beef cattle was managed the way his grandpa did it, and when it was time to take a few to market, he pulled an old wagon into town. He could fit a few steers in it, and still pull it with his farm truck.

When it was his time, Minnis died, and was buried next to his mother in the family cemetery. I heard later that the auction that followed was a strange one. His Shorthorn cattle and Poland China hogs sold for market price, bringing a fine net income. The furnishings in the old house were burned by the auctioneer, and his farm equipment sold for scrap. He was frugal in every way and lived his life in what most of us would call poverty. His neighbors felt sorry for this poor farmer. But when his farm with its streams and fields and rolling pastures was on the auction block, it sold for $1,600,000. Poor farmer?

I drove down by Minnis's farm the other day and there was a combine in the field.

Circling the Drain

There aren't any animals in this story, unless you count the humans. It's about the bathroom at our office, and if that doesn't interest you, just skip it and go on to the next story. It may not belong here anyway, given good taste and all, but if you want some further insight into life in the office, read on.

David Blaze is a master plumber. His father was a plumber and Dave has a key to our house. If we aren't home he can go in and fix whatever ails the water or gas works of a house built in 1888. He's creative, intelligent, and a client. He's been the guy to call since I bought the office over forty years ago whenever our kennel drains are blocked on the way to the sewer, or anytime his considerable skill is needed.

Our office line was plugged one day—the toilet wouldn't flush and the kennel was filling with water backing up in the drains. We called Dave and he came right over, took the "Big Eel" from his truck, and put it to work. An electric-motor-powered spinning cutter blade is sent down the drain, and with additional lengths added, can get the roots, sludge, or whatever happens to be causing the problem freed up all the way out to the street.

Dave used this tool at another house once, and when he wrote the bill he had included a charge for plumber's time, and another for the use of the "Big Eel." In Dave's handwriting, the word "Eel" looked like "Ed." The homeowner called and said, "I don't mind paying your bill, but I'm not paying this guy 'Big Ed.' I didn't even see him!" Since then when we tell Dave we need him to come over and bring "Big Ed," he knows what the problem entails.

Today it was raining outside and the access to the main line was out in the rain. Since access from the outside also required the attachment of several more lengths of spinning conduit, he tried to gain access to the sewer line by going down a large vent pipe in the laundry room. He and Big Ed went to work. The spinning blade would go down the pipe, and then make a turn toward the street in the Y intersection that his father put in the line in 1957.

As I was doing a morning surgery, the sound of Big Ed spinning away was replaced by a grating noise and the sound of shattering porcelain in the bathroom. Melissa ran over and opened the bathroom door. There, rising from the commode like the blooming silver flower of an alien plant, was

Big Ed's spinning blade, already two feet above the seat and climbing. She yelled, "DAVID, SHUT IT OFF!" over the sound of the machine.

Big Ed had taken a wrong turn on the trip to the street and come up through the commode. We all were thankful that no one was recycling their morning coffee at that moment.

Dave came around the corner, looked at the shattered toilet, and said, "We've done a bad thing." Apparently his father's hidden Y was a T, and Ed had made a right turn instead of a left.

But Dave had a temporary solution, since an office without this vital piece of equipment wasn't an option. Until a new pot could be ordered and put in place, he had two used models on his truck that he could install temporarily. We could pick one.

He opened the back doors of his truck and our options were revealed. Commode #1 had been taken from the Masonic Temple in town during its renovation. It was huge and not without fancywork—a toilet any Mason would be proud of. But since it was maybe a hundred years old and looked like it had been cleaned with a wire brush once during the Depression, we decided to look at #2. This was a modern style with yacht-like lines, long and low and screaming of design from the disco era. And it was chocolate brown, surely a popular color in a home filled with bell-bottoms, gold chains, and platform shoes. Far out!

We thought about our options for a minute or two, and decided we liked #2. It had been cleaned recently and had been replaced when the new owners of a home modernized.

We lived with that chocolate reading chair for what seemed like forever. Our clients who had pressing needs loved it. "What style! I love that color, Dr. Sharp!" Thomas Crapper would be proud.

But this isn't Walmart. We don't have a public "powder room" with a silver hand dryer, and a sign saying our piso is mojado. It's just a small room with a chocolate toilet, a small sink to wash your hands and, since it is also a darkroom, developing tanks for X-ray film. There's a dance that's done outside the room when X-rays are being developed in the darkroom and it's out of commission for ten minutes. This is always a time when someone is sure to have an emergency.

For a lot of years, Melissa and I were the only people who worked in the office, and the bathroom/darkroom was really not a public facility. But urgent situations occur, and when you gotta go, you gotta go. One such episode occurred when a longtime client went into the darkroom to see what developed, and after a while we heard, "Melissa . . ." And then a little louder, "Melissa . . ." I was just thankful she wasn't calling me.

Melissa disappeared and after a few minutes came out with our client, obviously upset. What went on in there? Well . . . in an effort to rise from the throne, the client had used the sink as a prop. Mounted to the wall in the fifties, the sink bracket stayed on the wall, but the sink came away and was now tilting toward the floor, ninety degrees from normal and held there by the water pipes and drain. So the woman called Melissa, and we called David.

The poor room took another hit one day when the morning surgeries were being dropped off. A woman pitched her cat carrier on the counter and hurried in the direction of the treatment area. "You got a bathroom? There it is . . . thanks," and the door shut. In a little while the woman poked her head out of the door and said, "Hey, Doc. You got a mop?" (You know it's going to be a stellar day when it starts like this.) Then she added, ". . . and a roll of paper towels?" As a matter of fact, we did have a mop and a full roll of paper towels.

When she left the office twenty minutes later, we drew straws to see who had to go in and deal with the wreckage. Surprisingly, the floor was spotless, the paper towels were gone, the waste can was empty, and the toilet flushed perfectly. Where were the paper towels, new and used? The bathroom was spotless. The mop was handed to Melissa as the client went out the door. The mystery deepened, so we sprayed Lysol all over the place . . . just in case.

When she came that afternoon to pick up her neutered cat, the client asked Melissa if she could use the bathroom again. "Sure, you know where it is," Missy said.

A little while later, she poked her head out of the door and said, you guessed it, "Can I have that mop again, and some paper towels? I'm real sorry." After a while she left, and when we checked, the bathroom was spotless. Maybe it's best not to know, but we all wondered. Exactly what went on in there—twice? How did she clean up so well? Was she a paper towel thief and this mop business was just a ploy, like the old story of the wheelbarrow smuggler at the border? I could waste a lot of time wondering, but I think I'll just flush it out of my mind.

Hollowtown

The city planner of Hollowtown must have had a hard time selling his vision to the city fathers because he ended up with something far less than his dream. Dr. Lukhart once told me that some people called it Stringtown. No matter what you called it, the town was now perfectly balanced. Two names for a town that had only two houses left. I knew the people in the brick house, but this time my destination was the other one.

Mary McClelland lived in Hollowtown in a white house with a small barn with horse stalls and a haymow. I was heading there to examine and hopefully eliminate a strange spot on her horse's nose. It was becoming unsightly and Mary wanted it gone. I found her house with little trouble since Melissa had given me explicit directions. "Turn left on Hollowtown Road after you've gone through Danville. Zigzag your way to Hollowtown and it's the white house."

I found it, and was greeted by Mary, standing in the driveway. "He's out back, Doc, and don't worry, he'll come to me when I call him. I haven't had him long, and the spot on his nose is about the size of my hand and growing."

Just as predicted, Cisco came when he was called, probably because he liked apples and Mary gave him a bribe. Standing before me was a large black American quarter horse stallion about three years old. He was a handful on the end of the lead shank, dancing and snorting, but Mary controlled him well considering her young age and inexperience with horses.

Looking at the top of a big horse's nose can be a little tricky. Usually you try to stand on the same side of the horse as the owner. If something you do spooks him, he'll jump away from you both, and it could take practically nothing to set him off. If you're on one side of him, and the owner is on the other, you can inadvertently send a thousand pounds of scared horse right into your helper. It's one of the first rules of dealing with an animal whose defense mechanism is flight.

I said "one" of the first rules. It's probably number two, because the absolute first rule is "Never stand directly in front of a horse." It worries me to watch a small 4-H kid stand right in front of his pal and throw the halter over his head and ears. A barn noise, a cat, a Kleenex, almost anything will scare a horse, and he could bolt straight ahead and trample the surprised teen. A horse was built to run, and flight from his enemies is the first means of defense. They're grazing animals and just like sheep or cattle, they're the prey of flesh-eating animals like mountain lions, or in the past, saber-toothed tigers. It's about survival.

If running doesn't work, and he finds himself in a bad spot, there are three ways any horse, mule, donkey, or pony will protect itself. His hind legs can kick backward if a perceived threat is getting close. A horse with steel shoes can do serious damage to a dog or predator with its hind legs, even while running, but accuracy is poor since the animal's eyes are on the sides of its head and way up in the front. If cornered, a horse can and will bite, and after carrying a hundred-pound head around all day on the end of a powerful neck, it's easy to see that lifting up the victim is no problem at all. Biting with huge teeth, then lifting and throwing the attacker is the second-best offensive weapon.

But a horse that really wants to hurt something or someone will strike with its front feet. This is more common in stallions than mares, and can be a way of asserting dominance as well. It's surprising how accurate a horse can be, flicking that big hoof up or bringing it down on a victim. Another reason to never stand directly in front of a horse.

The lesion on Cisco's nose was ringworm. It's commonly found on horses and can easily be treated with daily applications of medication. I went to the truck and in a few minutes was back with the anti-ringworm cream.

"Would you show me how to put it on, Dr. Sharp? I've never done this before."

"No problem, I'll put today's dose on." I opened the glass jar, put a dab on my finger, and reached up to rub it on Cisco's nose. Apparently he saw this as a threat. So he moved in a little toward me and then, with the accuracy and speed of a prizefighter, he went up in the air and struck the jar out of my hand with a hoof. I could swear I felt wind passing next to my right ear. He was down again and standing quietly before I could say, "Holy . . ."

I had violated Rule #1.

Mary was horrified. After I took a minute to compose myself, I said, "Why are you keeping a stallion? Are you gonna raise a herd of quarter horses?"

"Well, I just bought a mare and I wanted to breed her."

"There are plenty of stallions in the county you can use to breed her. He's too risky for you to keep intact, and in fact nobody really needs to have a stallion around as a pet. Let's geld him . . . right now while I'm here!"

"I've thought about it, and wondered why it hadn't been done yet. Sure, let's do it," Mary said without a moment's hesitation. I think it scared her to be around this aggressive guy.

In the next half-hour, I had Cisco asleep, gelded, and standing back up next to the barn with a calmer attitude on his near horizon. I got another jar of ringworm medication out of the truck and while he was still wondering how he got to the barn, I gave a detailed demonstration of its application. "Feed him an apple and talk to him while you do it. It really doesn't hurt. Just be careful, and have someone nearby—just in case."

On the drive to my next call, I tried not to think about what would have happened if he had swung that hoof an inch or so to the right. Maybe he aimed to miss.

Nobody Home

Nick Shaker was a huge man, well over six feet tall, and at least 275 pounds. He was an over-the-road trucker, and he and his Peterbilt had hauled loads to every corner of the United States and Canada. He was gone often, and to help pass the time, his wife, Frances, raised Pekingese pups. They were cute little squirts and it was always fun to give puppy exams and vaccinations to a new litter. I frequently saw the adults for eye issues, and the usual health problems that happen when a lot of dogs live together. Frances was a good client, a conscientious dog breeder, and a person whom we respected. I only met Nick once when I was making a house call to vaccinate ten dogs. He happened to be off the road and home for a few days, and I instantly liked him.

When we read in the *Times-Gazette* that Nick had died unexpectedly, Amy immediately said, "We need to go to the visitation."

Amy could have an audience with the Pope, and within five minutes they'd be talking about the dog he had as a boy. She can meet someone once, and six months later meet that person in an airport, and not only remember their name, but their pet's name as well. She takes an interest in people and they know it. It's a rare quality, but one that makes her the best possible person to greet clients, hear their problems, and put an arm around them when necessary. It was predictable that she would go to this visitation. It was her nature. I couldn't let her go alone, and since I knew Frances pretty well, I agreed to go with her.

According to the paper, Nick would be at the Yuhasz funeral home with visitation Friday, from five until seven. We could make it if we left the office after work, stopped to change out of our hair-covered clothes, and went directly there. I'm the opposite of Amy in some ways, not being as social, and had actually avoided funeral homes since I was a kid. My mother always said, "You don't need to go. It's not a place for you." I still thought that way as an excuse to avoid this uncomfortable situation whenever I could.

I finished with the last appointment and we left the office about 5:45. Amy and her family lived only a block away from my house, so I changed clothes at my place, picked her up on the way, and headed to the Shaker reception. After zooming down the hill five blocks and a left turn into the lot, we found a parking spot and hopped out of the Buick, adjusting our hastily put-on clothes as we walked. Amy grabbed my arm, and we hurried to the front door and a waiting Bill Yuhasz, the dour funeral director. We took our place in line. You've all done this—it's an awkward part of being a grownup.

The receiving line was long, stretching from the room with the casket out into the hall and down into the next room. We joined the line and inched our way along. As we finally made our way to the casket room and the family, Amy grabbed my arm tighter and said, "I don't see Frances."

I leaned into her and whispered, "I'm surprised a trucker would have a white casket!" Onward we inched and just as we reached the five family members standing by the casket, we could see that the person reclining on the satin inside wasn't Nick at all! Nick was bald, and we could see some gray hair on the pink pillow. The picture propped up at the foot of the casket was a woman, beaming out of a big chrome frame that said, "Resting with God—Blanche Something," and a date. We were about to greet a family of total strangers, and express our condolences about a woman we'd never met. This would take our best creative work! We kept our somber expressions.

Being the best talker, Amy went down the line first, and the middle-aged woman hugged her. I don't know what Amy said, but when the woman in black put the bear-hug on me I was speechless—rare for me. The next two men each gave Amy a big hug, and again I wished I'd heard what she said. I shook their large, calloused hands and nodded with a knowing look. I knew nothing.

The next woman introduced herself to Amy, so Amy turned and introduced her to me. She was Blanche's sister from out of town, so when it was my turn, and she said, "Did you know her before she lost her memory?" I had a little more information about Blanche.

"Not well," I said sadly, which wasn't a lie. "I hadn't seen her in quite a while." Which wasn't really a lie either, having not seen her in my entire lifetime, and that was quite a while.

The last family member, the one nearest Blanche, was clearly distraught and hugged me, thanking me for coming. We walked in a funereal manner to the front door, said goodbye to Bill, and made our escape. It could have been worse, but the family members were probably from out of town, here only for the funeral, and didn't know *anyone* in the line. That was my hope as we ran to the car.

"That was pretty weird," I said. "How did we have the wrong place? I read the obituary online." I'd never laughed after a visitation before—we knew we were going *straight* to Hell. Sitting in the car, we tried to compose ourselves. We were then on our way to one of the other two funeral homes in town, and we were cutting it close time-wise. The visitation at this place ended at seven and we had about fifteen minutes.

We pulled into the back of the Thomas Funeral Home and parked. This time we had more room to park since it wasn't as crowded. We hurried to the front door, pulled it open, and walked into the large front hallway. "No line here, I think we made it. Maybe we're late? There's a sign that will tell us which room Nick is in."

We walked to the back of the long front hallway and read the sign: "Jacoby Funeral—Private Visitation." Not only was Nick not here, but we had also just burst in on a private service for someone else. As we turned to make a quick exit, things got worse.

"Doc . . . Amy! Thanks for coming!" Appearing from the right side of the parlor was Jim Jacoby, a fellow Rotarian, and someone I had known for a long time. I had *no idea* what member of his family had died. Mother? Wife? Kid? Did he have a kid?

"Jim, we just wanted to stop in for a minute and tell you how sorry we feel. You know if you need anything you can call anytime. We don't want to interrupt. Please go back in." This was almost all true. We did want to stop in, we did feel sorry, and would certainly help him if needed. Jim thanked us for being so thoughtful. Otherwise we had just taken a swing and a miss for the second time. Nick wasn't here.

Since there are only three funeral homes in Hillsboro, we knew where Nick would be found. "Let's hurry up to Bolton's. He's gotta be there!"

As we drove by Bolton's Funeral Home all the lights were off. No visitation, and no Nick Shaker. Strike three. "What happened here? Maybe we were too late and it's over."

"Do you think we have the wrong night?" Amy asked.

"I don't think so, but we've been to all of 'em. Something's wrong."

I dropped Amy off, went home, and told our tale of the "Friday night funeral home tour" to Susie. She looked online, and said absolutely, the visitation was that night. A mystery.

I heard some commotion in the waiting room the next week and peeked out to take a look. It was Frances Shaker, and Amy was telling her how sorry we were to hear about Nick. Tears were streaming from Frances' eyes as she came through the swinging office gate and hugged us both. Amy said, "We wanted to come to Nick's visitation but we ran into trouble." Then she told of our night with total strangers . . . that we suspected that Nick probably wouldn't be in a white casket or have gray hair . . . of our intrusion into a private service, and our numerous ad-lib remembrances of the departed we had never met.

"Nick was at Yuhasz Funeral Home all right, but the one in Leesburg, not here. You were in the right place but the wrong town." And with that, she started to laugh. She laughed so hard that now the tears on her face were from hearing the story of our visitations. "I want to thank you guys. This is way better than seeing you at the funeral home. I haven't laughed in quite a while. Nick would have *loved* it."

As she left it seemed we'd accomplished what we'd set out to do Friday night. In a roundabout way we'd lightened the sadness of a client for a few minutes, and that was our goal all along.

"Gee, Doc, What Happened?"

I did a really dumb thing, and considering that I handle a knife for a living, inexcusable. I used an old scalpel instead of an X-Acto knife while building a radio-controlled model airplane. When the thin scalpel blade snapped, the remaining sharp edge stabbed me high on the back of my thumb, severing the superficial extensor tendon. I drove to the ER and was lucky enough to be there just as a hand surgeon was arriving. He fixed me up, and put my left thumb in a long splint. For a month.

Can you imagine how hard it is to work with your thumb in a big metal splint? No surgeries were possible, so we had to either reschedule the four or five surgeries we normally did each day, or send them to other local vets who were already busy with their own cases. About *eighty* procedures were reshuffled before it was over. Even giving vaccinations, which is about as easy as it gets, is a new challenge without an opposable thumb. You get so used to holding animals in a certain way that almost "one-handing" it was a real issue. Just as I was starting to learn how to do things this way, it got worse.

Reid, who was about twelve years old at the time, and I flew radio-controlled airplanes at a full-sized grass runway in Wilmington, Ohio. A week after my thumb-stabbing episode, when Reid's plane was about to take off, I noticed that the engine needed to be tweaked a little. I couldn't twist the needle valve with my left hand, the usual way, using my left thumb and pointer, so I did it with my right hand. This wrong-handed adjustment caused the knuckle of my right index finger to roll into the spinning propeller, and I got to meet my new best friends at the ER for the second time in a week for hand repairs. The doc on duty put fifteen sutures in the side of my right index finger, placed it in a straight splint, looked at the two of us and said, "Good luck, fellas."

With a big stiff wrap on each hand, daily vet activities posed new problems. It was hard to inject, pill, or even pet an animal. Just dealing with a zipper was a big deal, so you can guess what other jobs were hard.

Keeping my splints clean was easy, though. I wrapped them with vet wrap, and just changed it whenever it got dirty. Vet wrap comes in a roll, and is a stretchy two-inch-wide bandage material that sticks to itself. We had it in every color you'd want, including some decorated with dogs, cats, and chickens. We got the "discount color pack." My favorite was the white with blue lettering all over it saying OUCH! OUCH! OUCH! Sometimes I'd put red on the left, and green on the right like a boat, just because . . .

Now came the real problem. I walked into the exam room with the first patient, and the dog's owner said, "Gawd, Doc, what did you do to your hands?" I explained, and examined the dog. The next appointment in the other exam room said, "Gee, Doc. What happened to you?" The next appointment . . . and so on, until closing. Since I couldn't do surgery, we'd scheduled appointments *all day, all week*—some days twenty by happy hour. Every person wanted an explanation, except for Jasper Swingle, who sat like he was drugged and didn't notice, or at least pretended not to notice. We had a real problem here that needed a solution. The thumb splint was going to be on for at least four weeks.

Melissa had a great idea. We wrote a description of what had happened, and made copies for distribution to clients as they came into the waiting room. Do you think it helped? Fifty percent of our clients read it, and didn't ask what happened, but asked how I was doing with my new add-ons. The other 50 percent saved the sheet to read "later," and asked anyway. I was blessed to be showered with such concern, but I was wearing out.

Finally we found the solution. Melissa would say, "Wanna get a free office call? Don't mention his hands." Even that was not perfect, but I got a break for a while.

Mark Twain once said, "A man who first attempted to carry a cat home by the tail was getting knowledge that was always going to be useful to him, and warn't ever going to grow dim or doubtful." That guy probably ended up with hands like mine and like him, I certainly won't forget. Now, if a person comes into the office in a full body cast, wheeled in on a furniture dolly, do you think I'm going to mention it? Do you think I'll say, "Wow, Harry, what happened to you?" Not a chance in hell. Someone's already asked him that, and I'm sure he's already answered.

Wild Things

"And when he came to the place where the wild things are
they roared their terrible roars and gnashed their terrible teeth
and rolled their terrible eyes and showed their terrible claws."

—Maurice Sendak

Wild Things

The two young girls standing outside the small exam room were obviously upset. "The guy didn't even slow down. He looked like he was trying to hit him. It was terrible! He didn't even have the decency to stop," said the older school-age girl.

I nodded and asked, "How long ago was he hit?"

"Just a few minutes ago. We picked him up and hurried right in. Please see if you can save him. Mom's in there with him now."

"Well, let's go have a look," I said, and I started to push open the door to the exam room. Dogs or cats that are hit by cars are frequently left at the scene by motorists. Sometimes the driver's unaware that they have driven over an animal. Sometimes they're afraid they're in trouble, and just hit and run. Sometimes they just don't care. Whatever the reason, these good Samaritans had picked up the result of a car vs. animal meeting, and were kind enough to bring it to us for treatment.

As the door opened I was met by the pervasive, nauseating odor of decomposition and there, in front of me on the exam table, was the patient. He'd vomited whatever he'd eaten, and his feet and body were covered in goo. The people had been kind enough to bring to us an injured example of *Cathartes aura*—a turkey vulture. The "buzzard" appeared to have multiple wing fractures and was near death. He was breathing his last few breaths.

"I don't think he's going to make it, but it was kind of you to bring him in," I said as the youngest girl started to cry. "I'll take care of him from here."

The mom and her two girls left the office, at least knowing that they had done the right thing, and tried to help an injured animal.

When you look up in the sky and see the amazing ability of these birds to soar without effort, it never crosses your mind that they smell this bad. Their carrion-removal job involves a certain amount of pulling, tugging, and eating of dead stuff. Their feet always smell, and so does a lot of the rest of their body. It takes a real animal lover to pick one up off the road and seek medical attention. A wildlife lover.

We veterinarians are sometimes involved with animals that live in the wild. We may not have the same expertise with the wild ones that we do with domestic animals, but since MDs have chosen to treat only one species of animal, I guess the rest are left to us.

The next stories involve wild animals, and our involvement with them, however distant. They aren't stories of a vet saving Bambi, so don't get your hopes up, but rather situations we sometimes find ourselves in when dealing with nature. We meet "wild things" up a little closer than usual. Here you are . . .

Forensics

"Someone shot a bald eagle, and we want to catch him. Will you help us?" said the man in the green uniform. "We hate to just barge in like this."

I only knew one of the three men parading in the back door of the office. John Davis was our local state game protector. He wore a uniform and a badge, and carried a gun, and over the years he'd brought me a lot of interesting birds that were injured. Great horned owls, screech owls, and red-tailed hawks have all been passengers in his metal mailbox carrying-case. He was an animal lover and the perfect person to be a game protector.

The man behind him wore a different uniform—federal wildlife officer—and carried a large plastic bag in both arms as if he were carrying a baby. He introduced himself as Officer Dennis Quilty, and thanked me for helping them.

The third man was tall, pale, and wore a black suit, white shirt, and plain black tie. He looked like he had just walked off the set of *Men in Black*, and followed along. He said nothing, just stood there like a large black shadow. A little creepy. FBI? Lurch?

We walked to the treatment area where the bag was laid on the surgery table, and its contents were revealed—a dead juvenile bald eagle with a wound on its side.

"He was found in the southern part of Adams County by a farmer who heard a rifle shot," Officer Quilty said, "and he drove his four-wheeler out to investigate. The farmer had been watching a pair of eagles for months, and knew they had a nest down there somewhere in the woods. He found this young one under an oak tree, and called Officer Davis. Since shooting an eagle is a federal offense, he called me, and we started a report. We really aren't sure yet if he was shot, so John said you might help us. It's possible that he was injured in some other way, and died of natural causes. But I doubt it. That looks like a gunshot wound on his side."

"Lead will be easy to see if we take an X-ray. Even if a bullet went all the way through him, we'll probably see traces of lead," I said.

I took a few measurements of the bird, set the machine, donned my protective lead apron and lead gloves, and was ready to go. "Can I ask you fellas to clear the area? I can take these by myself, and I'd like you behind protective walls." They complied. I laid the eagle on his back and pulled both wings out to the sides—sort of "spread-eagled" (sorry). I fired the machine, switched film cassettes, and then placed him on his side to get a lateral view. I stepped on the pedal again, removed the cassette, and with the X-ray work done, I called the guys back into the treatment area, and went into the darkroom to develop our films.

He had indeed been shot. When we placed the 14" × 17" films on the view box a perfect, undamaged bullet was visible, entering from his left side, and lodging in his chest.

"Not much doubt about what killed him. I bet the guy who did this doesn't even know he can be fined up to $100,000, and sentenced to up to a year in prison! It's actually illegal to even keep an eagle feather," said my friend John Davis.

Officer Quilty spoke up, "Do you think you can remove that bullet without damaging it? It might come in handy for comparison later."

"Sure. I'll be careful not to put any marks on it." I laid the big bird on the surgery table, turned on the bright lights, and got the equipment ready. I put on surgery gloves, opened an instrument pack, and began to hunt for the fatal bullet. After some blunt dissection, I could feel a small hard object with my finger. A little more work, and I was holding a jacketed rifle bullet in my hand. I dropped it in an evidence bag, just like you see in the TV cop shows!

"This will be a big help in the investigation," said Officer Quilty. "We may never find the shooter, but we'll try. Can we have the films for evidence too?"

And off they went out the back door. The eagle had been placed back in his bag, and taken out to the green government truck with the investigators.

Months went by, and I ran into John Davis uptown at Pasquale's Restaurant. "Hey, John! Did you hear any more about our eagle?" I asked.

"Well, I heard a group of federal agents went down there and questioned all the people within a ten-mile radius. They spread the word that a big reward, maybe $10,000, was offered for information leading to the arrest of the shooter. Some of those hill-jacks would turn in their mother for that much cash. I think we'll hear something."

Almost a year passed. I'd pretty much forgotten about our eagle dissection when a different man in a federal wildlife officer's uniform came in the exit door.

"Just wanted to give you this," he said, handing me a manila folder. In it was a group of photographs taken at the time of the shooting showing the dead eagle, his wound, and ballistic reports on the bullet. "We turned up a suspect living in a trailer miles from where the bird was shot. Actually, the shooter's brother called us, and said he thought he knew who did it. We got a search warrant, found several rifles, and did some test shots. A bullet from one of the rifles was an exact ballistic match for the one you gave us from the bird. The guy knew we had him, and confessed. There's a letter in there from my boss thanking you for your help."

"Will he go to jail?" I asked.

"Nope. It was his first offense, and the guy was poor, but had a job, and was the sole supporter of his family. He was just out squirrel hunting, and took a pot-shot at what he thought was a buzzard. We explained to him that it's illegal to shoot them too. The judge threw as much of the book at him as he thought the guy could stand. Some fines, and community service I think. The best part happened as he was leaving court. He asked the agent-in-charge a question: 'Since I confessed, do I get the $10,000 reward money?'"

Woof

"You gotta be a little careful around him, Doc, he's 1/16 Timber Woof."

I'd heard this a lot over the years. I'd also seen 1/6, 1/8, and 1/32 woofs, and they all had two things in common: a shepherd-looking dog, and an owner with a great imagination. I'm not even sure how you could genetically make a 1/6 woof. Oh, and never a wolf, always a "woof."

I'd known James Free for nearly forty years. I'd hunted birds with him in Texas, had dinner at his home, shot trap with him in competition, and thought of him as a good friend. He stopped in the office one morning and said, "Rob, would you consider euthanizing a wolf?"

"Let's have a little more of the story here, James. What's up? Whose wolf?"

"My son's had a pet wolf for quite a while. He lived out West, and adopted this critter as an adult. He's a pretty big guy, around 120 pounds or so, and about seven years old."

"Is he really a wolf, James, or a wolf cross? We hear about these wolf-dog hybrids around here."

"Oh no, he's an Alaskan Wolf. I think another name is Yukon Wolf. He was used as a movie wolf in California, and when he wasn't useful anymore my son adopted him. He's really tame for a wild animal."

"Why are we putting him down? Is he getting aggressive or sick?"

"Nope, my son moved to Cincinnati and his neighbors are raising hell. They don't want a wolf in the neighborhood. They say he endangers their kids."

"Can't your son just say he's part dog, and tell 'em to step back?"

"When you see him, you'll realize this can't happen. He's tall, long, heavy, gray, and looks exactly like a wolf. We're at the end of our ideas."

"I assume you've tried zoos, rescue groups, wildlife rehabilitators—those kinds of places? Surely someone would take him."

"They say he's too tame to live in wildlife areas since he won't fit in a pack. Zoos are full—they don't want him. He's technically wild, so a lot of places have ordinances against him. He's a wolf that won't fit in anywhere."

"Check in with your son again and make sure this is what he wants to do. We'll think about it some more here."

"I know he doesn't want to put him to sleep, but he's being forced into a corner. The police are involved now, and he has a deadline in about a week. Call me if you get an idea." James left the office and I went on with appointments.

About four in the afternoon Leah Hufford came in the exit door. "Hey, Doc, do you know anybody who has a mean German shepherd or rottweiler they want rid of?"

"Why, Leah? You looking for a challenge?" Leah was a longtime shepherd breeder and could tame and train any dog. A mean dog might be such a test.

"Nope. We've been broken into for the second time by dopers looking for free pot. You know those two white buildings a couple of miles out of town on 138—the ones on the left with no windows? Those are mine and Jim's. First it was the cops. Buildings with no windows and using a lot of electricity—first thing they think is that this is a grow operation. Like we were raising pot in there under lights. And the place is surrounded by a six-foot privacy fence. So we gave them a tour and now they leave us alone. But apparently they aren't the only ones with that thought. Twice some lowlifes have used crowbars to get through the fence, bust the locks, and break in. My theory is that if I already have a big fence around the whole area, and I put a watchdog in there that will act crazy and terrorize unwanted peepers, maybe we would get some peace. Whattaya think?"

"I think maybe that would work, but you'll need to provide some creature comforts for the dog. He'll need his own enclosure with food and water, as well as daily care and the rest of the stuff you'd give your own dog. If he's mean, there's also a liability issue to think about."

"No problem, Doc. You know I love my dogs."

"I'll think about it, and if I hear of a dog like you're looking for I'll call you." I went home that night, and while I was watching the Cincinnati Bengals win a game, it occurred to me. If a mean dog would discourage a burglar, wouldn't a nice wolf?

I called James with my idea, and when he and his son were on board, I called Leah. "I might have just the 'dog' for you. Can you be at my office Friday at five-thirty? We'll see what you think."

James and his son pulled in the parking lot at five-fifteen and brought Romulus with them. When he came into the office on a leash I was frankly afraid of him. My God, he was huge. Super-long legs, tall, heavy (around 125 pounds), and wild-looking. He would certainly keep me on the other side of any fence! James' son said, "When he comes up to you, he'll grab your arm. He won't bite down, so don't freak out. It's like shaking hands in wolf-speak." Romulus came up to me, waist high, and quickly grabbed my forearm in his mouth. Just like the son said. He didn't let go.

"Oh, look, he likes you!"

If I wasn't pale, I should have been. I'd been around a lot of animals—crazy horses, mean mastiffs, wild cats (the scariest of all), bulls, and even a few owners that would scare you—but they were all predictable, and dealing with them was just a matter of experience and care. This situation was unpredictable. Romulus was no dog by a long shot, so when he let go of my arm, I sat down. He then sat next to me and put his head on my lap. Now it was apparent that he was tame, and used to people. But I could see why the neighbors in Cincinnati were afraid of him. He was going to be a great "watch-wolf."

Leah met him, fell in love with him, and said she would take care of him for the rest of his life. Everyone was happy with this.

I saw him at "work" a few times. He had a really nice building where he could relax. Lisa came out to play with him several times a day. He could run, walk, and sleep in his private yard, and got a lot of treats and good food. He wasn't *guarding* anything. It wasn't his nature. He just happened to live there with two buildings that had no windows. If you wanted to break in, I'm sure he'd greet you, but who in their right mind would do that? I vaccinated him regularly, examined him often, and cared for him until he could no longer stand. He lived to be eleven years old, which for an Alaskan Wolf is quite old. He had an interesting life, acting in the movies, living in a home with a human family, and finally having his own place in the shade working as a patrol "dog" for a couple who raised white mice in two buildings that had no windows.

I was never worried after that when some guy in bib overalls said, "You better watch out, Doc. He's 1/8 woof!" I knew the real thing—100 percent!

Quilled!

Vince is a hero. There isn't any argument about this. He wasn't just branded a hero by the local newspaper because he helped a cat out of a tree. He is a World War II Marine who, among his many other medals, was awarded the Purple Heart.

Most people who know him have no idea about his past, and I think he prefers it that way. Here's an example: I was responsible for providing the program at Rotary Club on Veteran's Day one year, and so I thought, "Who better to give a talk than a man who served his country in World War II?" Vince agreed to speak, and he told us about the Marines who raised the flag on Mt. Suribachi, Iwo Jima, and what had become of each of these men after their return to the United States. These heroes are remembered on the famous Marine Corps War Memorial in Arlington, Virginia. While his talk was fascinating, he *never once* mentioned that he was there! He was one of the Marines who fought on Iwo Jima, but true to Vince's character, he kept it to himself.

Vince is a devout man, soft spoken, and not given to swearing or strong language of any kind. When his church needed to select a new minister, Vince was picked as a member of the search committee, and he reads his Bible for an hour every night. So when I heard him swear at his dog and fire two shots from his shotgun in her direction I could make no sense of it.

Now I'm getting ahead of myself. You need to hear "the rest of the story."

Vince was getting older, and in his retirement he trained bird dogs and loved to watch them work. He was a bird hunter—quail in particular—and in the 1980s one of the best places to hunt these game birds was Texas. Vince would get permission from a rancher to park his camping trailer on one of the ranch's pastures (of 20,000 acres or so) and hunt the wide-open bird country of west Texas for the entire quail season. He paid the rancher by mail for this privilege, but the "pastures" down there were so huge that they never saw each other all season. Desolate country.

One day a good friend, and former Army Ranger who served in Vietnam, Jim Neil, stopped in my office while I was in the middle of the morning surgeries. "Hey, Rob. I just spoke on the phone with Vince, and he wondered if we'd like to fly down next week and join him for a couple days of bird hunting. Can you go?"

"Wow! I wish we'd planned this a little further ahead. My schedule is too full to take off without notice. I probably shouldn't." A long pause here while thinking. "Does it matter if we go over a weekend?"

"Nope."

"Well . . ."

Vince was the age of our fathers, but could walk after the dogs until our tongues were hanging down like red neckties, as a friend of mine once said. We both loved to hunt with him and who knew how often a chance like this would come. My schedule would always be full, and this was a rare opportunity to hunt with a man we both admired. So with some schedule adjustments, and without a lot of planning, we took Jim's English setter, Grace, our shotguns, some duffle bags full of clothes, and flew into Dallas. After renting a truck at the airport we drove half a day on a perfectly flat, straight, road toward the ranch in west Texas. Jim found an unquestionably creepy motel with a lot of vacancies about fifteen miles from the ranch. We dropped off our stuff, set out in search of Vince, and by the end of a really long day we were ready to flush the wild quail of Texas.

I'd always taken care of the bird dogs that Vince brought to the office, and Jim's dog Grace had been a patient since she was a pup. Since I couldn't bring a bird dog of my own (who hunts with a bulldog?), I would fill the niche of "dog mechanic" should the need arise. A couple days with these guys following some well-trained bird dogs in the heart of quail country was going to be a great experience.

The bright Texas sun materialized the next morning about an hour after we went to sleep, and lucky for us the motel had a "restaurant" that served breakfast: "Pancho's Hideaway." We took a chance—after all, the flies on the windowsill looked dead, and the next nearest place was hours away and maybe worse.

We parked the truck on the range, and let the dogs out to start sniffing and exercise a little while we put on our orange vests and got our gear together. The first thing I noticed about hunting birds in Texas was the difference in topography from Ohio or Michigan. It was vast. In the days of the Wild West, if the bad guys were on the horizon you might see their campfire, but never would be able to catch up to them that day. Here there were only bent little mesquite trees, small cactus, ankle-high grasses, and mostly flat ground that allowed you to see forever. After hunting over the dogs for hours, we could still look back and see the truck! Try that anywhere in the Midwest.

When a bird dog locates a covey of quail it freezes, and assumes the characteristic point that lets you know, "Hey, guys, here they are!" The other dogs will freeze to "honor" the point. Watching them work is fascinating. They run with their nose in the air sniffing, and all of a sudden they stop, silently yelling, "HERE!" When you move in front of the frozen dogs, the birds flush, flying up into the air.

Well, that worked pretty well until about four o'clock. Jim and I took Grace around one side of a small rise, and Vince and Marge went around the other side. Without warning we heard, "Goddammit, Marge, NO, NO! Goddammit." BOOM! BOOM!

I looked at Jim, who said, "I think he's shot Marge!"

"Naw, no chance, but whattaya suppose happened? I've never heard Vince swear before." We took off at a run around to the other side of the hill. There was Vince with Marge in his lap. Blood was everywhere on Marge's face, and it was easy to see she was hurt badly.

"She did the same thing last year! There must be five porcupines in all of Texas and Marge has to find one. She tried to kill it, and I just finished the job." Obviously the shots we heard.

I'd never been exposed to what happens when a dog attacks a porcupine. We never have that problem in Ohio, but without human help, the attacking animal will surely die. Marge couldn't close her mouth since hundreds of quills were inside, stuck in her tongue, her hard palate, her jaw, her lips, and gums. Her eyes were stuck shut with quills in the lids. Her cheeks and ears were covered in quills and because Marge had tried to dig them out, her front legs and paws were stabbed with hollow spines sticking out everywhere. The normally brave setter was limp and crying on Vince's lap with countless three-inch needles embedded in her body.

We were at least an hour's walk from the truck, and it would be getting dark soon. I had no anesthetic in the middle of an immense Texas ranch, and no instruments. But I did have two things that might make the job simpler—a SOG multitool on my belt, and an English setter—possibly the nicest and calmest of all the forty-pound dog breeds.

"Well, Vince," Jim suggested, "we still have a couple hours of daylight. Why don't we take Grace and hunt a while? We can stop and get Rob and Marge on our way back through here."

At first this didn't sound quite right—ditching us—but after I thought about it I said, "Go ahead, Marge and I will still be here. This is a one-person job anyway, and you'd just be watching. Just don't get lost." So off they went.

I sat with Marge on that Texas hill with the sun getting low in the sky, and went to work. She couldn't have been a better patient. She put her head on my lap and using the needle-nosed pliers on the multitool, I started to pull quills. It surely had to hurt. I started with her eyelids and after fifteen minutes she could see. I then pulled the quills from her stuck-open mouth, one by one. It seemed to take forever. Those in the back of her throat were the worst, but Marge practically held her mouth open while I grabbed each one and pulled. Porcupine quills have little barbs on them, so they don't come out easily. After an hour and a half Marge and I had had enough. Tears were pouring from her eyes, and if I didn't know better, I'd think she was crying. Most of the quills were out, it was getting dark, and I would be able to see any that remained better at the campsite. We lay back on the hillside and waited, Marge's head on my arm.

Jim and Vince came walking over the ridge with Grace running ahead, nose in the air, announcing their arrival. Marge was up and walking by this time and so was I. Back at the camper I took a few more short needles out of Marge's throat, but all in all, most were gone. And the next day, so were we.

Vince brought Marge into the office for a better look when he was back in Ohio months later at the end of the bird season. We gave her an anesthetic and removed a couple of quills way down in the back of her throat. To my amazement, she was really happy to see me. That was the first and last porcupine I've ever seen. Their reputation is well deserved, and so is the reputation of English setters as one of the best of all breeds both in the field and as a family pet.

Camping

Dr. Lukhart came in the exit door of the office in a sleeveless purple t-shirt, jeans cut off at the knees, and a pair of funny-looking sandals with the soles made from truck tires.

"What's up, Bill?"

"Martha and I are camping at the lake this weekend, and we wanted to invite you guys to come out. We'll make s'mores for Amy. Come on, you'll enjoy it!"

"Where are you camping?" I asked, since Rocky Fork State Park is a pretty big place.

"Come out North Shore Drive and turn at the sign that says 'campground.' Hard to miss. Come up the hill and drive 'til you see us."

Until that day my camping experiences had been pretty negative. When I was about fourteen, a buddy of mine, Glenn Miller, talked me into using my paper route money to buy a tent. He saw the green flyer in the paper that showed a beautiful wall tent on sale at the Fairway out on Route 422. We could ride our bikes the eight miles out there, but carrying a tent home on a bike would be tough. So we hiked, and by the time we got there by cutting through several housing developments, Steven's woods, and a cornfield, we were beat. Then we had to carry our prize home. This was no compact nylon wonder with telescoping aluminum poles like we have today. It was heavy canvas treated with a waterproofing additive, complete with wooden poles and stakes. It weighed a ton. When we got home, we drank a half-gallon of water, crashed on the floor, and could barely move.

The tent had a few characteristics that made it memorable. It was yellowish-orange with brown spots that looked like mildew, but I wasn't sure since I was just a kid. It had a distinctive odor that never went away, probably the waterproofing. On a sunny day, it could raise the temperature inside it by at least forty degrees. Oh, and at night, if it rained the stinker dripped water on us.

Camping out, I learned that sleeping on the ground like a cowboy allowed you to feel a lot of lumps in the grass that you couldn't normally see. My parent's happiest day was a Saturday morning when they looked out of the kitchen window and saw a dry tan square in the yard where the eyesore tent had been. Thieves had stolen it. Glenn Miller, the original brains behind the operation, went on to become a professor of philosophy at a prestigious university. His critical thinking must have begun later in life.

My other camping experience was provided by the US Air Force. If you fly, you have to attend survival schools—jungle survival in the Philippines, water survival in Florida, and everyone's favorite, a *week* in the mountains of Washington State learning to survive in deep snow. Why, you ask? There may arise a circumstance where you and your plane part company, and you and your parachute could land in the jungle of southeast Asia, the mountains of Nova Scotia, or the water somewhere. You never know. Let's just say that camping in a tent made out of a parachute, sleeping on a bed of pine boughs, and eating whatever you can trap or catch for a *week* in deep snow doesn't make you want to sing "Kumbaya." I survived, and that was the goal.

I wondered where Bill and Martha would pitch a tent in a park this big. When I found them I realized how little I knew. Why would two seventy-somethings want to sleep on the ground anyway? They didn't. They had a twenty-seven-foot Argosy travel trailer, a sort of painted Airstream. It was really cool and was in an area set aside for these big travel trailers. Their campfire was already burning and chairs were set up around it.

"Have a seat! Amy, we were just about to make s'mores. C'mon over here by the campfire and I'll show you how we do it," Martha said.

"Take a load off," Bill chimed in. "If you wrap a cover around it, I'll get you a beer. You can't have alcohol in a state park so if you cover the can . . . who knows? How's work?"

I sat down in a chair that rocked, and Bill handed me a camouflaged Bud. I leaned back and said, "I had to go down to Sugar Tree Ridge this morning to Jasper Swingle's place on Fair Ridge Road. He said he had a Hereford cow with pinkeye. When I got there it was obvious that his cow had squamous cell carcinoma. I told him that OSU could remove the eye and she'd be fine, that it was common in white-faced cattle, and if he wanted, I could make the appointment for him. He was going to think about it. Then I noticed white crystalline stuff all over the eye. I said, 'Jasper, what have you been putting on this?' He said '*salt*' like I'd caught him robbing a bank."

"Salt?" repeated Bill.

"That's what I'd thought. He said it was his father's cure for pinkeye. I guess it must make the eye tear so much, and the cow blink so much, that no normal microorganism could survive. Pretty brutal."

"Did it work?" Bill asked with a knowing grin.

"Well, since this wasn't pinkeye, all it did was make the cow more miserable. But it was cheap, and he's cheap. I told him not to do it again, and if he did have a real case of pinkeye, that we had better medicine now.

Salt thrown in an eye wasn't a cure for anything. Then he said I was making fun of his 'bleefs' and he didn't think that was nice. I said I found no fault with his 'bleefs,' that it was his science that was in error. He wasn't happy."

"My dad always had trouble at the Ridge too. He started practice in 1912 with a Model T Ford, and a trip to the Ridge and back took half a day. Well, one day he had a horse call down there . . . 'just not doing right.' So Dad went up to Lang's Smokery in town where the *News-Reader* is now, and thought he'd smoke a cigar on the way. He went in, bought a couple, and as he was leaving, ol' Harry Shanks, Marty's grandfather, happened to be standing there and gave him a free cigar. As he was about to get in the Model T, John Fender came up to him and asked if Harry had given him a cigar. Dad said yes, and John said, 'That jerk's been doin' that all morning. That cigar's loaded. Don't light it!' You might be too young to remember loaded cigars, but they have an explosive packed away inside. As it burns, it lights the powder and ka-blooey."

"I've seen 'em in cartoons," I said. "Go on."

"Dad put it in the breast pocket of his coveralls and headed to the horse call. When he got there, the locals had decided that the horse needed melted lard as a cure. There was lard all over the front of the horse, all over his face, and the town quack was covered too. He had a long beard covered with lard, and his hair was slippery, as well as his bibs. There was lard everywhere but in the horse. Apparently the horse was having none of it, wouldn't drink it, and by that time was pretty upset.

"Dad made a diagnosis—sick horse, I guess—got out his bucket, put some water in it, added some salts, capsicum, ginger, whatever he thought the horse needed, and as he did, the quack asked, smirking, 'Are you going to get him to drink it?' Dad just kept mixing. Pretty soon he got out a stomach tube, and just like he learned in school, passed it up through the horse's nose and down to his stomach. He attached a hand pump and pumped the entire bucketful into the horse without getting his clothes wrinkled. Everyone watched in awe. Dad packed up his stuff, pronounced the horse cured, and as he was about to leave, he pulled the loaded cigar out of his pocket, poked it in the quack's mouth, said 'No hard feelings—every man to his own work,' and lit the cigar. He got about 100 yards up the road when he heard BOOM. He was afraid to go back to Sugar Tree Ridge for quite a while!"

After we quit laughing I said, "Martha, can I make one of those?" S'mores immediately became one of my new favorites.

"Dad used that stomach tube a lot. I was always afraid I'd get it in the trachea and fill a horse's lungs with something."

"I was told that if you put it from the nose into the throat, shook the neck from side to side, and heard it bang back and forth, you were in the trachea, not the esophagus, and you'd better start over."

"Good theory," said the vet with forty years' experience, "but don't count on it."

Bill got a Bud out of the cooler, wrapped it in a hamburger wrapper (it was handy), leaned back and started another story.

"One of these days you'll meet my brother Ted. I came home from veterinary school one weekend and had a good night's sleep in my own bed. Before sunrise I heard this commotion downstairs and I asked my mom what was going on. She told me it was Ted getting up. The circus was coming to town, and he wanted to go watch them come in and get set up. Well, lunchtime arrived and Ted wasn't home. Dinnertime, still no Ted, and we were starting to get worried. We went to bed about eleven and around midnight we heard a truck pull up out front and Ted came in and went to my parents' bedroom. 'Where the hell you been? Just go to bed.' So Ted went to bed. In the morning Dad got up and went out the back door to go on a call, and there was a camel tied to a tree. Dad said, 'Where's Ted? What's this doing here? You have some explaining to do . . .'

"Ted told the circus people that since the camel was sick, his dad was a vet and could fix him. 'They gave him to us, Dad. Ain't he great!'

"Dad was a tolerant man, and used to things like this, so we asked a neighbor if we could use a stall in his barn and he said sure. He asked me what I knew about camels since I was in school getting a more recent education than his. I told him that I thought they could go a long time without water. Big help. He thought the beast needed a physic. Back then if you had no idea what was wrong with an animal, 'a good clean-out' was held in high regard. Camels have tusks, they spit, and they smell dead already, and this one was a good example of all of that. We finally got a rope halter on him, a stomach tube into him, and a 'good dose' of some of Dad's horse laxative was given. The next day the poor skinny camel was standing in the remainder of what those circus folks had been feeding him—peanut hulls, candy bar wrappers, some shiny thing we were afraid to touch—and he actually looked better. Ted and Dad were smiling.

"Over the next few weeks the camel gained weight. He had trouble chewing so Dad looked in his mouth and saw camel teeth. He had no idea what he was looking at, so he called OSU and got ahold of someone who was an expert. Remember this was in the late thirties and things were different up there. The 'expert' looked up how to age a camel, and Dad tried his newfound knowledge on ours. He determined that the critter in the barn was somewhere between real old, and real, real old, and was missing a lot of teeth. I guess that's why the circus was so quick to unload him. Anyway the neighbor who owned the barn where he stayed asked if he could feed him. Dad said sure, so the guy must have thought you fed a farm animal like a dog. He went uptown and bought a twenty-five-pound bag of calf manna, the richest stuff made, and dumped the whole bag in the camel's feed trough. Of course he foundered and died. I always racked it up to fate. The old camel was eating peanut hulls and dying of starvation in the circus. He died anyway, but at least he felt better for a while and didn't have to ride in a circus wagon at the end. All the neighborhood kids came over and had their pictures taken with him before the dead-wagon came. He died old and famous, and that's hard to beat."

Bill's stories went on until close to eleven. I especially liked the one about Bill's 8mm movie taken of Martha sitting on a rock in a creek when they were in the Smoky Mountains on vacation. He didn't want to warn her about the bear coming up behind her looking for food. It would ruin his great action film. He'd show it to me sometime. "Martha's still mad about that."

Amy was asleep in a chair by the fire. Susie was swatting some un-identified flying camp bugs, and it looked like it was time to hit the road.

"I have a whole new view of camping, Bill. Thanks for inviting us—g'night Martha."

"Next time I'll tell you about the cow in the well."

Since that night we've owned an Argosy, a pop-up, a Coachman, and two Airstreams. Camping has come a long way from my first night sweating in a suffocating, smelly canvas wall tent. I hope the thief enjoyed it.

Coon Huntin'

I've never been coon hunting on opening night of the season. Oh, I've been asked to go several times by clients wanting me to join in the fun. But if I went, someone else might be upset because I wasn't able to come to the office quickly. I get a call on opening night almost every year. When both you and your dog have been waiting for the season to start ever since the last one ended, you're both out of hunting shape. Hunting in the pitch-black woods all night long, chasing a critter over rough terrain with a portable head-light and battery pack is hard work. Fence cuts, foot wounds, eye injuries, and general signs of exhaustion are common. And the dog can get hurt too. About midnight I usually get my first call. I hate night calls.

"Doc, this is Denver Crawford. You don't know me 'cause I'm up here from Kentucky to see my brother-in-law Heber Collins. Really I came to hunt. Anyway, Flash and I was ahuntin' out in the woods by Heber's place with this other fella and his dog. I didn't really know this boy, but Heber said he had a good dog. Well, Flash got hurt, and I was awonderin' if you could see him."

"Do you know where my office is?" I always asked.

"Heber told me. Out by the stockyard, right?"

"Yep, and how long will it take you to get there?"

"About half an hour."

The usual. Too much time to leave now, but not long enough to go back to sleep. "See you then."

I was waiting when Flash and Denver came into the office, and it was clear that Flash had multiple wounds that were bleeding and dripping on the floor. Denver was a skinny old man wearing tan coveralls with a battery pack around his waist, a headlamp on his forehead, and a pistol in a holster on his belt.

"Let's get him up on the big sink here, Denver, and I'll have a look at him."

We have a stainless-steel sink about six feet long with a stainless grid cover. Anything messy is treated there so cleanup is easy. Denver walked his Redbone back to the sink, gave the rim a tap with his hand, and up jumped Flash. He landed with barely a sound and looked at me like I didn't think he could do it. He would have been right. I would have bet a thousand dollars he couldn't do that. No dog ever did that. I couldn't do that.

There he sat, with multiple punctures all over his neck and legs. When he stood up you could tell he'd been in the woods for a lot of years. He was swaybacked like an old horse, and the red hair on his face was turning gray. His feet, the size of coffee can lids, were flat and crusty, and the pads were cracked and hard. He looked like he could barely walk, but if he could jump up on the sink, he must be able to hunt. Flash!

"He's the best dog I ever had, Doc. I turned down ten thousand dollars for him once!"

There's an old coon dog joke about a guy who makes that statement. "I turned down [you fill in the blank] thousand dollars for him once," and the other guy turns his head to the side and says to his buddies, "That's where two fools met." In this case, Denver was definitely proud of his dog's prowess, and wanted me to know he was no average cur from the hills. Back then, coonskins went for twenty-five dollars apiece, and a good coon dog could tree four or more coons in a night. At a hundred bucks a night, it wouldn't take long to pay off a pricey dog.

"What happened to him? It looks like he's been in a fight. Did a coon do this to him?"

"Naw. It was that dog we was ahuntin' with. Flash got on the scent in a hurry and was mouthin' his way through the woods. I was afollowin' him, with this other boy and his dog fallin' behind. When I got to the tree, Flash was agivin' that coon the business, chewing the bark right off that ol' tree, tryin' to climb and howlin' like crazy. He got this here tooth because he likes to chew trees." He lifted Flash's lip, and his upper right canine tooth flashed back at me. He had a gold crown!

"Well, that old coon was up the tree just waitin' for me to shoot him out when along comes this ol' boy and his dog. That damn dog jumped on Flash and bit him all over the place. I ain't never seen the like. I grabbed the collars of both them dogs and pulled Flash outta there. I had to carry him back to the truck. He was whooped and I was mad."

I clipped and scrubbed all Flash's wounds, and since none of them looked too serious, I gave Denver some topical wound spray, and some antibiotic capsules for him to give Flash for the next week. We had a discussion about keeping Flash out of the woods for a while to let his wounds heal. I'm sure it went in one ear and out the other.

"Well, we might just as well sit down and wait," Denver said.

"He's fine. You can take him with you now," I said. It was after 1:30 in the morning, and I was ready to call it quits.

"I mean for the sheriff. He oughta be here soon. When that guy's dog hurt ol' Flash, I got so damn mad that when he came back to my truck to apologize, I jumped on him and gave him a whoopin'. When I left he was layin' in the ditch."

The sheriff didn't show up. Denver finally decided it was safe to leave, and loaded Flash by tapping on his tailgate. Of course he jumped right up and into his box. I was glad I never mentioned that stuff about "two fools met." I might have gotten the next whoopin'.

Evie and the Serpent

"If you hear a sound during the night, it's just the rattlesnakes. They're in the walls, and under the floor. Apparently they like the heat in there on these colder nights, and every now and then, I guess some of 'em have a disagreement. You'll hear 'em rattling at each other. Don't worry, they won't come into our part of the house."

"That's what he said, Doc. Do you believe that? I just talked to him on the phone last night, so I wanted to get my dogs vaccinated before we go down there for a visit. I guess when my brother wanted a cabin to 'get away from it all,' snakes weren't something he worried about. South Texas, just north of Laredo, has 'em year 'round."

"What's he do down there, George?" I asked.

"I really don't think *he* knows. He's the family member that no one has ever figured out. When the rest of us went to work in our dad's heating business, he volunteered for the Marine Corps, and this was in the middle of the Vietnam War. When he got out, he started a car repair business in his garage, and after thirty years, decided that he'd seen enough people, and moved to this place in Texas. He never married, but he's seen his share of girlfriends. He lives alone now, and asked if I'd come for a visit, and see his place. It sounded like fun, and I agreed to go down for a week. Then I heard about the snakes."

"I'll order in some vaccine for you, George. There isn't much call for it here in Ohio. Technically it's a pre-exposure vaccine against the venom of *Crotalus atrox*, the Western Diamondback, but you get cross-immunity against other species. We just don't see rattlesnake bites in Ohio often enough to keep the vaccine in stock. We see the occasional Copperhead, but dog bites from snakes are rare around here."

"I wish I hadn't told him I'd come now. I hate snakes. In the walls?— and under the floor? Aww, hell no!"

I ordered a box of vaccine and read the instructions. I had no experience with it, but my friend George had read all about it in a dog magazine. I called him when it arrived, and we vaccinated his two dogs—Evie, an English Pointer, and Monty, a Parson Russell terrier. We followed the instructions on the package insert, and before George and his dogs left for Texas, felt that we had done all we could to protect them. They probably wouldn't need it anyway. Dogs stay clear of snakes if given the choice.

"Can you give me a shot of that too, Doc? Just in case?" George said, almost as a joke.

"Have a great time down there. I hear it's really pretty this time of the year. You can tell me all about it when you get back," I said, trying to encourage him a little.

He did not have a great time down there. He called me on his cell phone as soon as he crossed the Kentucky border on his way home. "Can I drive straight to your office, Doc? Evie grabbed a snake, or the other way around, and it looks pretty bad."

"Come straight here. I'll wait for you," I said, hearing the panic in his voice.

His truck pulled into the parking lot about 6 p.m. and George and his two dogs came in the exit door. He must have driven from Texas like a stock car driver. He only stopped in a rest area once for a quick nap, otherwise drove straight through.

"Good thing you gave 'em those shots, Doc. We weren't there three days before Evie found a damn rattler sunning himself out behind the house. She'd never seen a snake that big before, so she went over to investigate. Before I could stop her, she was sticking her nose in that snake's face. He didn't like it—coiled all up, and started rattling like you see 'em do in the movies. Evie wagged her tail, jumped around a few times, and before I could say 'get away' that snake bit her on the neck."

"You'd think Monty would have been the one to hassle a snake. Terriers can't leave anything like that alone."

"It was all I could do to grab him before he got into the fight too. We were lucky there. My brother chased the snake away, and we went straight to some ol' vet in a dried-up town about twenty miles away. He was a cattle vet, and the first thing he asked was if she'd had the shot ahead of time. I told him that she was vaccinated. He said she'd either live or die, and gave me some penicillin pills for infection."

"I think his prognosis of live or die is pretty accurate, but we want to make sure it's 'live' rather than the alternative. Are those pills all you got from him?"

"Yep," George replied.

"Let's take a look at Evie. C'mon girl, hop on the table," I said, as I coaxed her onto the lowered mat of the electric lifting exam table. Up she rose, and I got my first look at what snake venom can do to tissue.

She had an area about the size of a baseball on the right side of her neck, where the skin had died, and was sloughing off. The major vessels were visible, along with the underlying muscles. The vaccine had allowed her immune system to be prepared for the venom, and protected her from the worst effects of the toxin—death. The wound looked like a cherry bomb had gone off in her neck, but she was alive, and actually fairly cheerful. Closing the wound with sutures wouldn't be possible or even advisable since daily cleansing would be needed.

I changed her antibiotics to a more modern drug, flushed the wound with running water, and had George watch, since this water therapy would need to be repeated at home daily. Gently running water would flush out the dying tissue along with bacteria and debris, and stimulate the formation of healthy granulation tissue (new connective tissue and microscopic blood vessels that form in the wound) necessary for healing a wound this large. Afterword, we sprayed a drug that was originally used to heal human decubitus ulcers (bedsores) into the wound. Evie was a great patient. It was frightening to think about what a snakebite could do to a human hand or leg.

I rechecked her weekly, and each time I saw her, the wound was smaller and closing together nicely. The pink granulation tissue was filling in the gaps, and Evie was acting like she felt well. After six weeks, I thought she was well enough to skip any further rechecks.

"Evie's going to continue to heal without any more help, George. Those last few inches will heal on their own. What do you hear from your brother? Does he still like his solitude?"

"I talked with him just last week. He met some girl that he thought was pretty nice in a bar down in Laredo. He invited her out to his place for a weekend visit. She was even thinking of marrying him and moving in, until one night she heard something in the walls of the house. He told her not to worry—they were just rattlesnakes and they were enjoying the heat in the walls. 'They'll never come into the house,' he said. Apparently neither will she. He's back to enjoying the quiet on his own—just my weird brother and his rattlers. I'll visit by phone from now on."

The Beat Goes On . . .

"The wise man must remember that while he is a descendent of the past, he is a parent of the future."

—Herbert Spencer

Into the Future . . .

After exactly one hundred years of going it alone, there are now two veterinarians at Hillsboro Veterinary Hospital to examine animals and consult about their problems. Sometimes it's just nice to look at a problem, and have the ability to ask another veterinarian, "How did she ever do that?" Or "Have you ever seen lab work like this?"

Modern cases have modern solutions, and I thought you might like a few stories from the present. They really aren't so different—they just happened at a different time. As I write this there is a rottweiler on the surgery table. She had her last litter ten weeks ago, and Melissa is prepping her for an ovariohysterectomy (spay). In the waiting room is Mary McQueen, waiting for her appointment with Beignet—a Frenchy, and a soft little ball of dough. Bloodwork on a diabetic Manx cat is being run in the Catalyst One chemistry analyzer. Amy is helping someone at the counter, Maddie is helping Reid gown up for surgery, and all's right with the world. Until the next emergency . . . here we go . . .

Magic

"Nnnyyessss, this is Wilma Main, and I have a dog that needs a C-section."

Those same words came over the phone like a recording, and I must have heard that recording a dozen times. The phone always rang at 3 a.m. and the voice was always the same, like that bad dream you have over and over. She never gave a warning in daylight hours, or a simple statement in the afternoon that her dog was in labor. Just the dreaded, "Nnnyyesss, this is Wilma . . ." and always at night.

Wilma bred Boston terriers and her dogs were show dogs—beautiful, with blocky heads, which put them into that category of "probably needing a C-section" with every pregnancy, like a lot of Bostons. This was never a surprise to her, but it was somehow always hidden from me until the last minute.

As an aside—there are three words here that intrigue me when we speak of cesarian sections. The first is that we always say, "They had to *perform* a C-section." Magicians *perform* magic, and take a bow. Musicians *perform* a piece of music, and take a bow. Does this mean an audience should be waiting, and a bow taken, outside the delivery room? Next, *cesarian* seems to be an antique word that goes back a long way, since it's based on the Latin word *"caedare"*—to cut. No one really knows for sure if Julius (or his mom) had anything to do with such a delivery. And *section* . . . what's with that? No other common surgical procedure is called a *section*. Sometimes we section, or cut up some tissue, but the procedure isn't called that. We never hear, "I'm going in for a gall bladder section," or "Frankie just had a quadruple bypass section." An attempt at a surgical delivery used to just be called an "operation" until a book was written in 1598 calling a similar procedure a "section" and it stuck for some reason. So now, instead of "delivering puppies surgically," I was going to "perform" in the middle of the night.

There are several problems with doing a C-section at night. Most obvious is the fact that you have no office staff there to help you, and the dog owner is rarely of any use. During the surgery, which is almost like performing magic, you have an anesthetized patient in front of you, and pretty soon you might have six or eight patients to care for. For one person, this is tough.

Next, you might be using two or more sterile surgery packs of instruments that will need to be cleaned up and re-sterilized that night before you go home, because they'll be needed for the next day's planned surgeries.

The surgery table and floor are always covered with fluids and some blood when you're done, and will need to be cleaned up for use the next day. Mopping the floor is a skill that is rarely considered an essential part of a surgeon's work, but for country veterinarians, it's pretty common. Surgical drapes, those cloth or paper barriers used during surgery, will need to be replaced and sterilized too.

And then, of course, after working from 3 a.m. until everything's done at 6 a.m. or so, you have just enough time to go home, shower, get dressed, and go to work the next day, having been up since you heard the dreaded, "Nnnyyesssssss, this is . . ."

But this time I had help. Reid was going to be my assistant and things would go much more smoothly. We were waiting as Wilma's Blazer pulled into the office parking lot, headlights shining against the dark building. The plump woman in an oversized blue running suit fumbled in the back seat, lifted out a gigantically swollen Boston terrier, and came in the unlocked exit door of the office.

"Good morning," I said, as she rushed passed me.

No response to that. "This will be her third C-section, Doc. You delivered seven last time, and I'll bet there's more in there tonight. She's really big."

Reid took the leash and walked "Bonnie" back to our treatment area.

"Call me when she's done," Wilma said as she turned and went out to her Blazer, whose engine was still running. I watched as her taillights pulled out onto US 50, heading back toward Coon Crossing. No help there, as usual.

"Where should we start?" Reid asked.

"I'll take her back into the kennel and give her a pre-anesthetic while you get out the packs. We'll need the large surgery pack, a drape pack, an extra pack of sterile 4 × 4s, a blade, some 0-Vicryl suture, some 00-Vicryl, and a pack of size 7.5 gloves."

"Got it," Reid said as I took Bonnie back into the kennel and gave an injection of pre-anesthetic. This drug is used to allow us to give a lower dose of other anesthetic drugs. I put her in a cage while the drug was being absorbed, and then came back to the surgery area and got out an appropriate-sized endotracheal tube, some IV fluids, and an intravenous catheter.

I looked around and said, "We'll need about four towels to work on the pups. Can you get those, and I'll get a bottle of Dopram ready for you to give the pups?" Dopram is a respiratory stimulant and a couple drops on the tongue of a newborn will help a lot with breathing. Reid would act as catcher tonight. The "catcher" stands behind the surgeon, and as each pup is removed from the uterus, his job is to remove any remaining membranes, clear the airway, rub the pup with a towel to stimulate it, and give Dopram on the tongue from a pre-filled syringe. He's called the catcher since, for the sake of sterility, I would drop each pup into his toweled hands without touching him. You can see why working alone is tough, and an assistant (with good hands) is very valuable. If I had to stop to resuscitate each pup, and then change into another pair of sterile gloves, the mom would be under anesthesia much longer. Reid would take care of the pups, allowing me to concentrate on the mother with the huge incision.

"Let's get started!" I said. We put Bonnie on her chest, and Reid held off (plumped up) the vein in her front leg while I placed the IV catheter. I started her fluids, gave the next anesthetic drug, and while Bonnie went to sleep, Reid held her mouth open while I placed an endotracheal tube and hooked her up to a gas anesthesia machine. We attached all the vital-sign monitors, rolled her on her back, and while I was scrubbing and putting my sterile gown and gloves on, Reid clipped the hair, and put a sterile scrub on the area of Bonnie's abdomen where I would "open her up." We were ready, and so was Bonnie.

She was huge and a long incision was necessary to exteriorize the uterus. We actually take the big y-shaped uterus full of pups and place it up, out of the abdomen, and onto a large drape. (It's okay—it's really still connected in there.) This allows fluid and blood to run onto the table and not pour back into Mom's abdomen as each pup is born. Each pup is float-ing in fluid that runs out as the pup is removed. I counted eight lumps in the uterus and could see my previous incision. Eight pups this time—a lot for a Boston.

As I dropped each pup into Reid's waiting hands, he cleaned it up, gave it Dopram, and rubbed it 'til it was mad enough to start squealing. We had an incubator once used for baby humans that was plugged in, and nice and warm. As each pup was ready, Reid placed it inside. By the time I started to close Bonnie up, Reid had eight black and white Boston pups crying in the incubator, ready for dinner! Bonnie should be very proud.

I started the process of waking Bonnie up, and called Wilma to come and get her and the new litter. Apparently she had gone home, and was asleep when I called. Reid had taken all the instruments we used and put them in the sink to be washed, re-packed in their order, and sent through the autoclave to be made sterile. He was ahead of the game. I started the cleanup process on the surgery table and put the towels in the washing machine. When Wilma finally arrived, Bonnie was awake, the pups were ready for travel, Reid had the packs in the autoclave starting the sterilizing cycle, and I had mopped the floor. We had about another half-hour of work ahead of us, but were making good time.

Wilma came in the exit door and in her usual brusque manner said, "Eight pups, huh. That's a pretty good litter. How much do I owe ya?"

We settled up, I gave her medication to take home, and we prepared the gang for travel. As I got Bonnie up and moving, Reid went over to the incubator to get the pups, and put them into the box that Wilma brought. "You better tell that kid to be careful!" she said. "I wouldn't want him to drop one. They're valuable, you know!" I didn't have to look at Reid to know that his eyes were rolling.

And so another night of magic was performed. One dog was placed on a table like a magician's hat, and eight dogs were lifted out. Eight beautiful pups that would grow to have different futures. A few became family pets, a couple were average show dogs, and one little squealer who would become both an American and Canadian champion.

Reid got a chance to see into the future for a few hours also. He would do it again many times in the years to come, and that wasn't the first time he'd helped me. It's just that it was a Friday night, and he didn't have to get up for school the next day. He was only ten at the time—in fifth grade—and he could sleep in the next morning. His own first C-section would come sixteen years later delivering bulldog puppies for Dave Madison. He didn't drop one of those either.

Career Beginnings

"Doc, on the 16th of next month we're having career day at the high school. I know you've always come in the past, and I hope you can make it again this year. Can I sign you up?"

"Absolutely. Can I bring my dog?"

"Clipper? Sure! We look forward to seeing you both."

I love these programs. Unlike Jr. High Career Day, where you're in a gym with a lot of other occupations, on High School Career Day you actually sit at a table in a quiet room with eight students at a time, and talk about a career—in my case, veterinary careers. Most kids know my job, but not other veterinary opportunities. Our County Health Commissioner, who is a veterinarian, is an example. Some counties even have coroners who are veterinarians. Some vets are engaged in scientific research, and some teach at universities. The military loves to "hire" veterinarians, since they manage the food services at all posts and bases, and unknown to most folks, all of the meat in the country with a "USDA inspected and approved" stamp on it was inspected under the supervision of a veterinarian. You can be an equine specialist and practice exclusively on racehorses, or only treat exotic birds if your interests lie there. A classmate of mine is a veterinarian at the St. Louis Zoo, and another friend practices at Sea World—very specialized areas of the profession. And speaking of specialized, there actually are honeybee practices with bees as their only patients. The jobs available are wide-ranging and not restricted to practices like ours. I've found that most high school students have no idea about these other areas—they think that all vets are "animal doctors."

The one question from students that's become tougher to answer as time passes is, "How can I become a vet?" That answer isn't so clear. Most of us never knew in high school that we would become veterinarians. Most of us never knew in high school *what* would become of us.

Universities offer a variety of courses that most high school students never knew existed. Business courses like accounting and marketing, science courses like ornithology, entomology, and geology, liberal arts courses in philosophy and religion, social sciences like psychology and anthropology, courses in computer game design, and so on. Any of these may be career paths if tried. Biology and chemistry courses to upper levels will be required for admission to vet school, but may not be courses some students like once they're taken. Pre-vet classes really don't have a lot to do with live animals.

The history common to all veterinarians is that we studied what we liked, got good grades in what we studied, and didn't stop until we eventually reached the end goal. Advice for students in any field, really. Our son Reid had that rare combination—a love of animals that all veterinarians have, and a gift for studying science. His grades were exceptional and his interests were clear. He applied and was admitted to "vet school." His mom and I were very happy!

Reid was finally done with nine years of university education. He'd been gone from Hillsboro long enough that a lot of folks forgot we had a son. He had passed the state and federal tests to become accredited, and the state and federal tests to become licensed, and was finally given permission by those in authority to see his first patient. He walked in the back door of the office ready to go to work, was handed the records of "Bruce" the cat, and I said, "He's in the small exam room—you're on." He was about to see his first appointment as a graduate DVM.

The owner of Bruce—a new client—was a "Reiki Master," as we were told. Reiki is a healing technique based on the principle that the Master can channel energy into the patient by means of touch, activating natural healing processes in the patient. This can be done with the healer's hands placed above the patient as well—not touching anything. Bruce was on the exam table for euthanasia. He was very old, very sick, and at the end of his ninth life. Reid was told by someone in the room that not only was his owner a Reiki Master, but *so was Bruce the cat*. Knowing nothing about this alternative method of "healing," Reid pressed on, and asked the human Master to sign the required permission form for euthanasia. Bruce looked like he would appreciate it, lying flat out and motionless on the exam table. There were five other Reiki practitioners in the exam room as well, all crowding around the exam table, and all ready to help with energy healing—or whatever else should the need arise. They brought music.

It has always been our feeling that a dying cat shouldn't be disturbed more than necessary. Euthanasia should be entirely pain free, with as little hassle as possible. We give a quick injection of an intramuscular anesthetic, and the old kitty simply goes to sleep. This is followed by an IV injection of euthanasia solution that is never felt. That way, if there is any difficulty finding a vein, which in an old cat can be a challenge, it's never painful. Reid gave Bruce the anesthetic.

The five practitioners, one in a flowing robe, two in jeans and tank tops, one in a glittery pink top that said "Pink" on the front, over studded leather motorcycle chaps, one in an ill-fitting flowered dress, and the Master wearing shorts and her Reiki t-shirt, all held their hands flat out in front of them and six inches over Bruce. They were saying things in unison that none of us could hear, including young Dr. Sharp, who was squeezed out, a little back from the ceremony. Bruce was sleeping peacefully, unaware of all of the energy that was aimed in his direction. After a few minutes, Reid interrupted the energy performance, and finished the job. The Practitioners took Bruce home for burial, and things went on as usual in the office.

"How do you like it so far?" I asked Reid whimsically.

"Did you save that appointment just for me?" he asked.

"Actually, I didn't. They made the appointment for euthanasia of an eighteen-year-old cat over the phone—no talk of Reiki. It was just your luck!"

As the weeks progressed, Reid fell into our office routine easily. When people called the office and said, "Dr. Sharp told me last week that . . . ," we needed to stop the conversation and say, "Which Dr. Sharp—mustache or bow tie?" We discouraged the differentiation by age, since one reply was "the elderly one." She's off my Christmas list.

After a couple of weeks one of our clients gave Reid a gift when she was leaving the office. After a journey that led him through all those years of formal education, and a student debt that will follow him for a decade, he's arrived back where he started—not in the city practice where he spent two summers working with city vets, but in a town where people know him. A town where a young client thought enough of him to give him a gift—a name tag to wear on his lab coat: "Dr. Cupcake."

Serenade

Reid spent two summers when he was a veterinary student observing and working in a large city practice. Some cities have veterinary hospitals with twenty-five veterinarians or more, and a staff that includes technicians and assistants numbering twice that many. No client ever sees the same vet twice. No practitioner sees the same client or patient more than once unless by accident. There may even be several locations through which these staff members rotate, so repeat appointments with the same veterinarian are impossible. Reid had a great opportunity to see some exotic surgery, expensive equipment in use, and was given an eye-opening view of city life. But he didn't get to see a client get out an electric guitar and perform for the waiting room until he came back to our office in Hillsboro.

Just as with country doctors, our clients and patients get to know us, and we develop attachments to each other over the years. I see the children of clients as adults—all grown up. Frightening as it sounds, now I see their children as third-generation clients with their pets. Many are Reid's age and are quickly developing a relationship with him and Amy that I had with their grandparents forty years ago. Small towns are like that.

So when Mr. Williamson appeared in the doorway and said, "I thought I'd give your clients a treat today—a little serenade," we certainly couldn't say no. The appointments that afternoon were with clients and patients we knew well, and might enjoy his act. Or not.

He set up a microphone, amplifier, speaker, and sandwich board with his name on it in the business area, so he "wouldn't be in the way" and tuned up. An amplified guitar in a small office can be quite impressive—and loud. He got ready to perform as Amy put clients in each exam room.

Eloise Johansen went into the large exam room with Pete, the Parson Russell terrier. Eloise was a woman in her seventies who had grandchildren in the same grades as Amy's sons—my grandsons. We were old friends. We closed the door, and Eloise was describing Pete's scooting issues to me as we heard the sound of feedback screech from outside the room. I greeted Pete on the exam table, had a quick look around his constantly moving body, and asked if it seemed like his scooting was getting worse.

"Last night he was really miserable, Rob. He alternated between scooting and licking. I think he seems a little better this afternoon."

I looked under his stubby tail and saw a swollen area at about the four o'clock position on the anal clock. It was open and bleeding. "No wonder he feels better, Eloise. He has an anal sac abscess and sometime recently it popped open. That relieved the pressure and eased the pain. Problem solved, except for clearing up the infection. Let's check the other anal sac." I put on a glove, lubed the appropriate finger, and promised Pete it wouldn't hurt a bit. Just as I started to check the other sac, Mr. Williamson announced, "For my first number, I'd like to sing 'The Bell's Foundry Blues,'" and Pete jumped. I held his tail and Eloise said, "Isn't Joe a hoot? I didn't even know he could sing."

We finished with Pete. I gave Eloise some instructions about hot-packing the open abscess, sent home some medication, and as I opened the exam-room door, Joe concluded with, "She was hot as molten metal, and I thought our love rang true, but it seems her bell was ringing for the chief of the night-shift crew." Followed by applause from the waiting room. We were losing all control.

I went into the small exam room to hide, and to see Mabel Wilson, Amy's second-grade teacher thirty-five years ago. Her cat, Precious, just needed her annual exam and vaccinations. We talked a little bit about the office entertainment, and how Mabel had taught Joe's son in the second grade, quite a while back when the Rainsboro school was still open. They say that music calms the savage breast, but Precious must not have been a music lover. As soon as "Never Pick Your Tattoo When You've Had Too Much to Drink" was in full swing, Precious jumped down from the exam table, ran for her carrier, and disappeared inside. She was ready to go home. Unfortunately I hadn't vaccinated her yet, so I lifted her carrier up on the exam table, reached inside, and in a minute she was ready to get in the car. Mabel said, "I heard Joe perform at the Senior Citizens Center last week. He can go on for hours." Hours?

I went back into the other exam room now and greeted Denise and Harry Falcone. They had a farm in Folsom at the top of Folsom Hill. I'd taken care of Harry's cattle until he decided he'd retire from the cattle business and just do some grain farming. He was seventy-five, and could still easily climb up into a combine. Denise made cherry pie that was the best I've ever tasted. We talked about crop yields that year, and the crazy price of equipment. Harry said he just bought a tractor that cost as much as he paid for his farm forty years ago.

"I think Benji's been limping on his left rear leg, Doc. It's hard to tell sometimes. He's pretty active and when he's running you can't notice it at all. When he gets up, he really feels it, and then gets better as he walks. Kinda like me!"

Benji was a cross dog. He wasn't a mean dog, but a cross between just about every dog that ran the Folsom hills. Medium size, medium hair, medium black with a little white trim, and friendly. He could ride on top of the toolbox that stretched across the back of Harry's truck for any trip to town or any trip into the fields. He had great balance, and if you saw him uptown on the toolbox when Harry was parked at the bank, you could yell "Hey, Benji!" and he'd wag his tail. As he got older I always expected to fix a broken leg when he slid off his spot and onto the road in a turn. So far, so good, though.

I examined him and said, "I think he has arthritis in his hip, Harry. Let's take a quick X-ray and see." We snuck past the entertainment to the X-ray machine during a break in the singing as Joe wet his whistle with a Mountain Dew.

Benji's left hip showed some arthritic changes that were probably causing the pain. The right hip wasn't as bad, but was going to be a problem soon. We started Benji on anti-inflammatory drugs, and had a talk about riding *inside* the truck. I was worried about his ability to stay up on his perch as he aged. Harry agreed.

Just as Denise and Harry were heading out the door, and Amy was putting the next appointments in the exam rooms, Joe's break was over, and he began a tune that may *never* have had electric guitar accompaniment in the years since it was written. I could be wrong. Betty Buckley must have felt a chill when her classic from *Cats* was undertaken. "Memory" sung by a retired trucker with an electric guitar was begun, and the occupants of the waiting room were fascinated. Just as Joe hit the high part, there was sudden silence, and the lights in the front of the office went out. The lab computers whined down, the air conditioner was silent, the windows provided the only light. A circuit breaker had given us a sign—enough music.

With our entertainment at an end, the schedule went back to its normal pace. Joe Williamson would have to perform at the Senior Citizens Center where they have more power. Apparently we just couldn't handle it. I bet one of those big-city practices with all the exam rooms and all the space could have enough power. But then Joe's not their client, is he? Thanks, Joe. You help keep routine from the door.

House Call

How hard can it be to vaccinate a cat? In a standard five-hour afternoon we could hypothetically examine and vaccinate four cats in an hour, or twenty total, if all were healthy, and if Melissa could actually schedule this many cat appointments in an afternoon. This would never happen of course, since we also see dogs, emergencies, and animals that require bloodwork, X-rays, and more time than just healthy cat exams and vaccinations. All you need to derail any schedule is to have a truck pull up with a Great Dane that was just hit by a car. But it isn't hard to vaccinate a cat, and about fifteen minutes would be time enough.

Maude Henderson's cat Millie took longer. She made her appointments by mail for starters. As Maude aged, her hearing started to get a little strange. "I can hear everything people say. It's just that they mumble their words. They need to speak more clearly," she would say.

The mumblers increased to include almost everyone, and since they mumbled on the phone as well, there was no use trying to deal with people using a phone. The mail worked perfectly well. This was the start of Millie's appointment—a written request for a house call "somewhere between March 6th and the 9th, in the morning between 9 and 10 a.m. at her place on Bent's Camp Road, on the south side of the lake, just one drive past the mailbox that looks like a bass."

We don't usually make *house* calls for a single cat, by mail or otherwise. If a client had several cats, or a disability that made an office visit difficult, I would go to their house. One cat, about half an hour from the office, means that if everything went perfectly, you would still blow half the morning for a ten-dollar vaccination. Do you really want to charge an elderly client a large trip fee to give a single poke to her kitty? I don't think so.

But I liked Maude Henderson, so I told Melissa to write her a note and say I'd be there. I'd mail it at lunchtime. What's the benefit of owning your own office if you can't bend a rule now and then?

On March 9 at a little after 9 a.m. I arrived. I should say *we arrived* because I always take Amy on house calls. She loves to go along. She's been around animals all her life, is very social, and can converse with anyone. And she's a lot more agile than I am—if someone needs to climb, dive, grab, or find a cat, she's the best.

In the office, I place the cat carrier on the exam table, open it and voila!—the cat. In a house, people rarely have their kitty in a carrier. "Don't worry, Doc. He'll come when I call him." That almost never happens.

Maude's house was a double-wide mobile home. Well, that's not exactly true. It was a single-wide placed laterally on the lot, with another single-wide right in front of it and joined to it. Two mobile homes . . . a double-wide. We could hear her TV from the truck, and getting louder as we walked up to the front door. Mrs. Henderson was waiting there, always smiling and pleasant. It was one reason we enjoyed seeing her. She invited us inside.

Immediately we noticed that she was a collector. Inside the front door to the left was her doll collection. What had been the living room of the front trailer was now reserved for a large family of over a hundred "baby dolls." There were no stuffed animals, Disney characters, or Beanie Babies. These were the pink-faced, big-eyed, blinky babies, with styled hair and dresses or nighties on. Baby dolls—all looking at us. Now I collect a lot of things, some of which people might think strange. And I believe that going full-out with a collection, a crazy excess of something—the stranger the better—can be a good thing. The man who covered his entire house with bottle caps is someone to congratulate. I just wasn't used to having all those eyes looking back at me.

The TV was almost deafening inside, and the people on the show were absolutely not garbling their words. Not a mumbler in the bunch. Since it was early March, the heat was still on, and as I've gotten older I appreciate heat, but I wasn't ready for this. My parents thought that when their house hit eighty degrees it was about warm enough, and this trailer would have been to their liking. It was even warmer.

Mrs. Henderson collected Tupperware in the next room. From the floor to about five feet in the air, and six or eight containers wide, and three or four deep, was one of the finest gatherings of burp-able containers Amy or I had ever seen. Remarkable.

Every double trailer has two kitchens, and you only need one to cook meals. She filed bills in the sink of the first kitchen in a very efficient manner, and used the other kitchen, in the other trailer, for cooking. I could only imagine what was stored in the first kitchen fridge. It wasn't plugged in, so . . .

The front door of the second trailer, in the middle of the merged pair, led us to her living area. The TV was there with a group of women talking over each other so loudly that the neighbors in the mobile homes fifty yards away could enjoy it. Overstuffed furniture was arranged in a conversation grouping. Millie, the ginger patient, was sitting on the back of a pink divan, looking at us as cats do when they suspect something is about to happen. Debbi, our office cat, would jump down, walk over, and say hello at this point. Not Millie.

To our right, at the other end of the room, was a plant collection. Pots on the floor, tables, stools, and chairs filled with cactus plants, violets, sprouting geraniums from stems kept over the winter, orchids, and plants I'd never seen before, were packed in under the window at the end of the trailer and spread six feet or more into the room. Cat litter and potting soil were intermingled.

Millie leapt from the couch and threaded her way through the plants to her first defensive position next to a cactus. Remember my office example of the exam table—open the carrier, pet the cat? This wasn't even close. Cats are smart and don't always like a stranger clomping around in their space. Many prefer to hide, freeze, or disappear and watch to see what's going to happen. Millie had picked a good spot from which to consider her options.

Mrs. Henderson called her. "Millie, kitty, kitty, kitty, want a treat? Come see what Mommy has for her baby. Come here, sweetie, see what I have for you, kitty, kitty, kitty."

Millie stared. You could almost hear her think, "Do I look that stupid?" But you couldn't hear *yourself* think over the TV women arguing. Man, it was hot in there.

Amy tried to approach from behind. She can catch a cat in a mid-air leap if necessary, but Millie snuck between the flowers and ran for the babies out in front. Mrs. Henderson tried to catch her but no luck. "I really didn't think it would be this hard." They all say that.

We went out front and there, between Betsy Wetsy and Chatty Cathy, sat Silly Millie with just her face showing between the babies. Obviously she knew she was the target, and whatever it was—she wanted none of it. Mrs. Henderson climbed on the divan that held eight babies and our girl, only to watch her burrow under Madam Alexander's finest, and appear behind a baby in a pink tutu. From there Millie hit the ground, and like a shot disappeared back into Tupperware heaven. We followed. We thought it might be a good idea to surround her, and then close in on her. If she ran then we could grab her. This is no way to deal with a cat, by the way. They like a chase, always win, and are incredibly good hiders. You're better off trying to lure them with kindness and soft tones. The loud TV made that impossible.

Mrs. Henderson made a great effort to snatch up Millie and missed, then fell into the Tupperware, and onto the ground. Tupperware fortunately makes a great soft landing pad. She was a slight woman in her eighties, a fine Tupperware bouncer, and a good sport with a fun spirit. We stopped the chase, helped Mrs. Henderson up, and assessed the situation. Tupperware was everywhere. We thought we might chase Millie into the bathroom and catch her in that confined space. She avoided the bathroom. Back and forth we chased, with no luck at all. I know the ginger speedster enjoyed this. She was, after all, a redhead.

On one pass, Amy caught her running by the plants, and as she attempted to scruff her and slow her down, Millie dug her claws into Amy's thighs and jumped. Not being held in a good grip, she escaped and headed toward the plants again. This wasn't Amy's first cat wound.

All's fair in a good cat chase and apparently the chase was getting to Millie. As she ran into the plants this time she stopped. Nature called, and the plant dirt seemed like a good spot to an upset cat with nervous diarrhea. As she assumed the position, I leaned over a few African violets and jabbed her in the rear leg. She was vaccinated. Mrs. Henderson was happy. Millie glared.

The trip out and back took an hour. The chase took about an hour. Having cookies and milk with Maude afterward took a little while too, so all in all we made it back to the office in time for lunch. But we vaccinated Millie, and she was good for another year. Mrs. Henderson sent us a thank-you note—in the mail, of course.

My Turn to Worry

Sometimes I think I'm guilty of seeing serious illnesses as challenges to be won or lost, without remembering that a very worried and upset owner is involved as well. Veterinarians don't always think of what it's like to face the loss of a very special friend, and be unable to do anything about it. When you're an animal lover, the chances are great that you will get your turn. I did.

By now you've read the story of Clipper. You know he became my dog, and you've been told what condition he was in when Big Alex brought him to the office. What I didn't tell you was a problem that popped up over Christmas when he was five years old. Reid was home from veterinary school for the holidays, and everything was in full celebration mode. Our three-story Queen Anne was showing off her five-color paintwork with white lights and pine roping, and we were preparing for a lot of partiers.

"Do you think he looks right?" Susie said. "When he came in from outside he just stood there and stared at us. I think something's wrong with him."

She was referring to Clipper, of course. I told you he was 100 percent trustworthy around strangers, and he'd been exposed to a zillion people over the past years, never acting excited. On one visit to a nursing home a man wearing a football helmet ran at him and whacked him in the face, and he just stood there. A dog this stoic doesn't give you a lot of clues when he's sick. Pain was something he once had, and endured like few other dogs. "Standing there" was kind of his style.

"Did he eat today?" I asked.

"I'm not sure he's eaten for a couple of days. His short friend there might be cleaning up some of it," Susie said, referring to our other dog, Stella the Scottie, low and bold.

So Reid and I took Clipper over to the office. His physical exam was normal, but he had a mild fever, and his bloodwork showed an elevated white cell count, and nothing else remarkable. Since these were signs of an infection, we started him on antibiotics and went home to Christmas turkey and Jack Daniel's punch.

But he didn't improve. I'm not a patient person, although I've told people over the years that you have to give the drugs a chance to do their job—five days at least or maybe longer. I wanted him better right then, so after three days we took him back to the office and checked him out again.

His temp was higher and his white cell count was rising—worse. Now I was worried, but we changed antibiotics to a big gun that rarely fails, and added a second antibiotic to cover the spectrum. A "gorillacillin cocktail."

As New Year's Day approached, with Clipper still standing like something was bothering him, Reid and I checked him again. He was no better, and his fever was higher. It was time to call in reinforcements—an internal medicine specialist who had been on the faculty at OSU when I was a student, had been in private practice in Cincinnati for more than thirty years, and was a close personal friend. I had referred tough cases to him for as long as I had been in practice. Maybe Bill could sort this out. He was a wizard with ultrasound and since our X-rays gave us no clue, I hoped he might be able to solve Clipper's problem. He lived near Hillsboro, and attended the Presbyterian Church along with our family.

What do you say when you call a vet about a sick dog on New Year's Day? I've heard the same speech from clients for decades, and now the words were coming out of my own mouth. I took a deep breath and placed the call. The call always starts with an apology: "I hate to bother you on a holiday" is always the first step, so I tried it. "But my dog is really sick" always follows. Then you usually hear, "He's been sick for a week but today he's really bad." That was true here as well, but I had the advantage of labwork and vet-speak, as if that made such an interruption in Bill's life less of an imposition. He listened as I told the story, and I think he could tell I was really concerned.

"How 'bout I come over to your office so you and Reid can fill me in. I'll take a look at Clipper myself. Fifteen minutes?"

"We'll be there. Thanks so much, Bill." Wow, this was better than I'd hoped. His skill was recognized over the whole tristate area. The best diagnostician that I knew would be looking at our dog in fifteen minutes. Reid and I put the big sick guy in the back seat of my truck and headed to the office.

Over the course of the next few hours we did tests on joint fluid, spinal fluid, abdominal fluid, blood, and urine. We took X-rays of areas that were suspicious, and palpated every inch of him. Bill agreed that an infection was present but we couldn't find it. Sometimes we see this with malignancies. Our plan was to continue with the antibiotics one more day and when Bill's practice in Cincinnati opened on Monday, he would ultrasound Clipper's abdomen. Could we take him there? You bet. Bill went home to his family gathering, which included his son from out of state who was only home for two days. That's a good friend and a dedicated veterinarian.

Now a series of complications arose. On the morning Clipper was to go to Cincinnati, it was snowing and accumulating, six inches or more. It was about an hour and a half to Bill's practice on a dry day. I had four surgeries and fifteen appointments of my own scheduled for that day, so it would be up to Reid and Susie to take him to Bill. They started early and took their time. On the way, Reid stopped to help the driver of a car overturned in a ditch, and was told by an oncoming semi driver to go back and take a different route. The road was closed up ahead. By noon they arrived after a crawl along a six-lane road and a slide into the parking lot. We always carry a lot of weight in the back of our truck and four-wheel drive can help with deep snow, or an off-road adventure, and it was helpful here as well. The snow was letting up as they parked and helped Clipper inside.

While I was seeing patients I got a call from Reid. "We found an anterior midline mass in his abdomen on ultrasound. It has fluid in parts of it and seems attached to the liver. Bill says it looks bad, but without an exploratory, he can't tell. He wants to know if you want to do the surgery."

"What's the alternative?" I asked.

"Bill says the surgery can be done right here. The senior vet is an excellent surgeon and is willing to take a look."

"That would be my preference," I said, coming up with a number of reasons why I'd rather not. If euthanasia would be needed, they . . . well let's just say I wanted Paul LeFever to do the surgery . . . and without delay.

For the next hour I was seeing patients wondering what was happening in Cincinnati. After another hour my phone rang. It was Reid.

"Paul asked me to scrub in with him. He's still working but I thought you'd like to know—it looks like a gall bladder mucocele, distending the tissues to several times their size and attached to a lot of other tissue in the abdomen. Paul's sitting down for a few minutes to rest. He's not sure we can get it out, and we may need to take out part of the liver. Even if we do, Clipper may still die."

The good news was that it wasn't cancer. The bad news is . . . well, you already know. So I asked Reid, "What does Bill think?"

"I don't know. He's in an exam room seeing the patients that Paul was supposed to see. One of Paul's clients came in and wanted to know who the new guy was. Mom told her that he was an internist filling in while Paul dealt with an emergency. 'So I'm getting an upgrade?' she said. Mom thought that was a riot." One of the best internal medicine referral specialists in Cincinnati was squeezing anal sacs and treating ear infections! That's a friend! So I went back to work squeezing anal sacs and treating ear infections at the other end of the line, waiting for the next call. It was another hour, and it was Paul this time.

"Hi, Rob. I really enjoyed meeting your son. He was a big help with this. I usually like challenging cases and this was a tough one. We got the mucocele and gall bladder removed along with a lobe of the liver and a lot of mesentery and omentum [the Saran-wrap like tissues that hold the works together]. I was able to save the ducts and now he just needs to recover. I'm sending him home with Reid and your wife. He might as well recover there as here. Three things might happen. He might bleed out tonight and die. He might die from the stress of all this. He might survive and take a week or so to get any strength back. Let's keep him on his drugs and I think we'll add another one as well. Call me tomorrow and let me know how he's doing. Stitches out as usual."

What followed were a lot of thank-yous, and a short talk with Bill. It was dark now for the trip home and the roads had been plowed and salted. Reid carried Clipper up the back steps of our house, and laid him down on his favorite rug in the kitchen. He was out of it for quite a while, but I sat next to him, with a hand on his head. He would do the same for me.

He lived. This was the afternoon when I saw patients in my office thinking I'd probably never see my own dog again. I'd always thought that we needed to treat the critter on both ends of the leash or our job wasn't complete. But until I became that worried owner—with the helpless feeling that my best pal was slipping away from me, and I couldn't do anything about it—did I fully realize the situation that some of our clients face. Bill, Paul, and Reid bailed me out of a gloomy place with a willingness to help, even over a holiday. Reid learned both the technique and perseverance that it sometimes takes to finish with one in the win column. But I'll always remember the day when an old friend, and a new one, and our son accomplished what I couldn't, and gave me back my "perfect dog."

Double Whammy

Some busy afternoons I'll see clients in one exam room, while Reid sees clients in the other. It's much more efficient this way. Reid poked his head in while I was examining the McKelvie cats, and said, "When you get a chance, will you come look at this dog?"

The English setter on the table in the other exam room was beautiful. She was mostly white with black splotches all over her body, and stood like a show dog. "Check out her abdomen," Reid said, as Amy held her on the table. Her owner, a thin man in his sixties, sat across the room and watched quietly.

Her abdomen was distended and tight, and the dog was in obvious discomfort.

"I'd like to take her in the back and do some labwork. Can you see clients in both rooms for a while so I can find out what's wrong?" Reid said.

"Sure, no problem," I told him. "Let me know if you need help."

So I continued our routine appointments while Reid took Sarah, the setter, to the treatment area. Mr. Winyard, Sarah's owner, wouldn't be needed for a while, so he went across the street to the Dairy Queen. We could reach him on his cell phone.

Reid and Melissa drew blood, and in twelve minutes the computerized blood analyzer's printer spit out a CBC and profile. While Sarah's serum chemistries were only mildly abnormal in a few parameters, her blood count told the story. She had a white blood cell count of over 60,000, with a normal WBC count in the 8,000 to 10,000 range, and contained mostly neutrophils, with the other white cells mildly elevated. She was anemic as well.

So an unspayed female with a swollen abdomen and a super-high white cell count usually points to one problem—pyometra. They took Sarah over to the X-ray table and took a look, and the digital image showed the full abdomen and tubelike uterine structures typical of pyometra. In dogs, pyometra is a sterile abscess of the uterus—a collection of white cells with no bacteria—brought on by an imbalance in hormones, causing the normally Y-shaped structure to fill up, and swell, occasionally to ten times its normal size. The dog then becomes toxic, the kidneys begin to fail, and the dog dies. Without surgery, Sarah would die. In about twenty minutes, modern technology had given us a diagnosis and course of action that would have taken much longer only five years ago.

When he returned from the Dairy Queen, Mr. Winyard came to the treatment area where Reid showed him what he'd found, and recommended surgery at once. Every hour that passed would allow Sarah to become more toxic, and possibly die. It was a risky surgery, but we had no choice. He agreed.

I continued to see clients in the exam rooms while Reid gave Sarah the preanesthetic. In about fifteen minutes Sarah had an IV catheter in place, was asleep on her back with an endotracheal tube in place, and hooked up to an isoflurane and oxygen gas machine. She was connected to a monitor that showed her blood oxygen percentage, heart rate, ECG, temperature, blood pressure, and respiratory rate on a big screen that was easy to see during surgery. If things started to go wrong, at least Reid would be tipped off early.

The surgery was begun, and after a while Melissa poked her head into the exam room and interrupted my viewing of Lori Swaddles' cat's ear. "He wants to see you," was all she said. I thought trouble was brewing. Reid didn't usually need me during surgery.

I walked back to the surgery area and there on the counter, spilling over on two sets of drapes, was a nine-pound uterus, a whopper. "Glad you got it out without having it rupture. That should make her feel better," I said.

"Come over here and take a look. We have bad news," Reid said through his mask.

I looked down into his incision, and I could see the reddish-colored, knobby texture of a tumor. She had cancer as well. "Wow, that's not good. What kind of tumor is that? Can you see where it's attached?"

"I was just so surprised when I found it that I told Missy to get you. It looks like it might be part of the spleen. It's huge. I can't get my hand around it."

"Well, that would be the best-case scenario. Why don't you feel around it, making the incision as big as you need? If it's the spleen, maybe you can get it out. She doesn't really need the spleen anyway. If it's not the spleen, she's in real trouble. We can ask Mr. Winyard if he wants to wake her up if it's terminal." Reid agreed, and I went back to the exam room, and Lori's cat.

I was about four appointments behind and trying to catch up when Missy came and said, "Come look."

On another set of drapes covering the counter was a huge spleen with a softball-sized mass at the distal end. It weighed about eight pounds. You can do without a spleen or a uterus, by the way. "I had to enlarge the incision from the sternum to the pubis to squeeze this out. She's lost some blood, plus the blood in the spleen itself, so we hung some more fluids. Do you believe that? If she hadn't had pyometra, we might not have found the cancer. Two organs gone, and she's seventeen pounds lighter. I'm going to look around now that there's more room to see in the abdomen. Just to make sure there aren't any other surprises in there."

"Amazing. I've never seen that. A double whammy! Good job! I bet Mr. Winyard will be happy."

He was. The incision was closed in the usual manner and after a day of rest, intravenous drugs, and fluids, Sarah was eating and went home. She came to the office to have her staples removed two weeks later, and Sarah's family could not have been happier. She was a new dog. Thanks to laboratory equipment that can give results in minutes instead of days, digital X-ray technology that gives beautiful images in seconds, modern anesthesia and monitoring unavailable a few years ago, and, I should add, surgical skill, a dangerous pair of disease problems was discovered and cured in less than two hours. And both in the same dog!

Pyometra and splenic malignancies existed in the past, and I wondered how interested and amazed Dr. Lukhart's father would be if he could watch this afternoon's surgery. Two fatal problems, probably untreatable in his time because of the lack of diagnostics and quick action, fixed at once. How cool is that?!

Walking with Bill

Animals are always finding new ways to challenge vets, and if it isn't by some mechanical wizardry—like getting their head stuck in a Mason jar—then it's with a new presentation of an illness so rare that textbooks only have a line or two describing the signs. It makes practice challenging, fun, and the best job any puzzle solver could ever hope for.

What do you do when you don't know what to do—run into a puzzle you can't solve? You can't turn to the back of the book for the answer like you did when you were a kid. Now, I refer the case, as mentioned earlier, to internal medicine specialist Dr. Roger Williams. He was Bill to his friends. Like the rest of us, he's a puzzle solver too, but unlike other vets in private practice, Bill works on the problems that we can't solve. When we give up, we pull out Bill's phone number.

I ran into him in the hallway at the Midwest Veterinary Conference during a break for lunch. We have four days of continuing education lectures by some of the best specialists in the country at this meeting every year. Veterinarians from most states and even some foreign countries attend. I was there to learn, and Bill was there to teach.

"Hey, Rob. How's everything in Hillsboro?" he asked.

"Under control when I left. I hope to get a little crappie fishing in yet this weekend. You should come over! We can have the boat on the water in twenty minutes!"

"Boy, I wish I had time. I'm involved in a new project at a hospital in Cincinnati. An oncologist, who's using lasers on certain types of cancer, asked me if I'd like to be in on the research and have some dog patients with cancer participate, so I agreed. It's important new research, and we should get some great data. We're giving our patients a porphyrin—a form of chemical that's taken up by certain types of cancer cells. You've heard of porphyria—the disease that makes people have to stay out of the sun. These chemicals are activated by light, so when they settle in the cancer cells, and we activate them with the light of a laser, bingo, they cause the cancer cell to die. Photodynamic therapy might open a lot of new treatment options for some cancers and other metastatic diseases, so I've been smuggling some patients into the laser lab. You can imagine what some patients might think if the patient ahead of them for treatment was a basset hound. The hospital prefers that the less people see of the dogs we bring there, the better.

"You'll like this though—after a few weeks of sneaking small dogs in under coats and in gym bags, we had a thought. We had a young black

Lab that had a perfect cancer for our study, but was too big to stick under a coat. We had to pass through quite a bit of the hospital on our way to the laser laboratory, and everyone would see us. But who would notice two guys in scrubs pushing a gurney down the hall? We just needed to have our Lab asleep and covered up. Since she was a pretty big girl, we decided that a morgue cover would be the perfect concealment. A dead body on a gurney was not an unusual sight in a big-city hospital."

"Did it work?" I asked.

"Perfectly. At least for the first few weeks. We had a system. We gave the Lab an injectable anesthetic in the back seat of our car. The laser technician and I would then lift her onto the gurney, place the morgue cover over her, and make our way through the hospital to the lab. Anyway, it was about eight in the morning one day, and we wheeled her into the elevator, but before the door closed three members of the cleaning staff squeezed their way in. These were pretty big women, and five humans and a gurney really filled up the staff elevator. The elevator started up, and between floors, Gracie, the Lab, started snoring under her morgue cover. Dead bodies shouldn't snore. One woman turned around with eyes as big as ping-pong balls. My quick-thinking technician made a snoring sound and started blowing his nose. One housekeeper quickly pushed a button, and they couldn't get out fast enough at the next floor. You could hear them all talking excitedly outside as the elevator went back in motion. I wonder what they said! We laughed all the way to the lab. Eventually, after a few months, we just walked the dogs in like therapy dogs, and no one really cared. People just wanted to pet them."

"I still remember how once, many years ago," I replied, "when I was a vet student just passing through the treatment area, you had a dog on a table, anesthetized, with an endoscope down his esophagus. You had students all around you, and you called me over to take a look down the scope. The dog had been brought in for chronic vomiting, and I expected to see some mysterious lesion in the wall of the stomach. I took a look, and there, looking back at me from the dog's stomach, was Mickey Mouse—the centerpiece from a one-year-old's birthday cake. Mystery solved." (It would be another thirty-five years before our son would surgically remove Disney's Lumière from the intestine of a dog—equally decorative, and also from a birthday cake.)

"Let's go down to the cafeteria and get some lunch. We have about an hour break," I added.

"Okay, but I do need to get back by one o'clock to hear a friend of mine give a session about our responsibility as veterinarians to treat pets as a way of helping humans. She thinks that we shouldn't treat dogs or cats just to make them well, but to help keep their owners healthy, too. She works with a lot of PTSD patients, and isn't a vet. She's a psychiatrist."

"She might be interested in the story of a client of ours—Larry Cornwall," I said as we walked the long halls of the Columbus Convention Center, our name tags hanging around our necks. "I'd known him for at least twenty years. He wasn't like most of our clients because he had cerebral palsy. He couldn't drive his dog to the office, so I always made house calls. Larry was placed in a 'home' as a baby, and ignored—along with a lot of other kids with disabilities. Back in the forties they had no idea what some of these kids could do. Larry was never taught to read or write or even brush his teeth 'til he was removed from the home as an adult.

"He learned to read, write, and speak, and was eventually treated like a human with a very sharp mind trapped in a body that gave him no cooperation at all. He loved to do woodworking, and everyone wanted his six-sided picnic tables. He could sell them as fast as he could make them. His dog, Taco, was always with him. When he sat, Taco was on his lap. When he slept, Taco was on the bed, and when he used power tools, Taco sat on Larry's empty wheelchair, and waited for the noise to end. Taco didn't care that Larry was different, or that his speech was different. Dogs don't understand most words we say anyway. So you can imagine when Taco got old, and we found an abdominal tumor, how panicked we were—not so much for Taco, he was fifteen, but for Larry. He didn't have many friends, and he was about to lose his best one.

"When Taco died, Larry found out how many friends he actually had. He had offers of puppies from every corner of the county. Larry was resolved never to get another dog. He said he would become 'too attached.' One day, he stopped making picnic tables, and spent most of his time in his wheelchair staring at the TV. Sometimes his caregivers would see tears on his cheeks, and knew he was missing his little pal. They called us to give us updates.

"Several months later an elderly client of ours died, and her out-of-town adult children wanted nothing to do with her long-haired Chihuahua, Ben. He was about seven years old, perfectly house-trained and healthy. I'd given him his puppy shots and cared for him all his life up until then. The out-of-towners thought the solutions to their problems were simple: bury Mom, auction the furniture, list the house, euthanize the dog, split the money. We didn't care about the rest, but Ben wasn't going to be a part of their scheme. Amy took Ben off their list of things to do.

"We called and asked Larry's caregivers if we could come over and talk to him—we had a job for him. They said sure, anytime. Amy and I went over to his house and I knocked on his door. Larry greeted us with his usual ear-to-ear smile—'Doc!!!' he said, greeting us like long-lost friends. We went into his living room and sat down.

"'We have a problem and we hope you can help us. Some people want to put a little dog to sleep. We said we'd take it, but now we need a foster home—for a while anyway. Are you up for it?' He looked surprised, and wasn't smiling anymore. Had we made a mistake? Amy left for a minute and came back in the front door with Ben. She put him down, and he walked across the floor and jumped up into Larry's lap. Wow, what a salesman! I'd forgotten his previous owner used a wheelchair at times.

"Larry's smile was back as Ben curled up in the same spot on Larry's lap that Taco had occupied.

"'Can you keep him for a while, Larry? You'd do us a real favor.' He nodded and his tears were back.

"Larry died in his sleep a few years later, just before he turned eighty-two. Ben was on the bed with him. After his new pal arrived, Larry had gone back to his shop in the garage and started to make picnic tables again. He was happy again. After his death, one of Larry's caregivers took Ben home with her. I guess Larry actually did 'foster' Ben until he found a new home. It just took a while."

Homer

No one wanted Homer. His adoption fee was "reduced." It said so on his cage as he sat in the parking lot of the plaza waiting with some other dogs who were all hoping to be adopted. They were brought there by a rescue group, and they'd brought Homer there several times before. Nobody wanted him then either. The cute beagle puppies went fast. The Lab was gone before he was even out of the truck, but not Homer. Barney, the big muscular pit bull, found his home last weekend. No one even petted Homer.

Maybe it was because he was an adult, about seven years old, and people wanted puppies. Maybe it was because he was funny-looking. His head was a little too big for his body, and of course there was the eye business. His right one was gone, removed a while ago, leaving a jagged scar. Or maybe it was because his jaw stuck out and his lower teeth were always exposed, bulldog style . . . or those huge ears. Whatever the reason, the little white Chihuahua-cross sat looking out of his cage at the people playing with the other dogs. Always the other dogs.

Our daughter Amy was a grownup now with a husband and two boys. Ever since she was five years old she had ridden with me on farm calls, and as I took care of the sick animal, she played with the kittens in the haymow. She helped hold cow leads that were wrapped around a tree a few times, and loved to play with the dogs and cats in the office kennel. She never met an animal that was so dirty, so sick, so hurt or neglected that she couldn't pet it, hand-feed it, or just make it comfortable. When little girls in her class played with dolls, Amy played with stuffed animals, and when she went to college, she lived in a house most of her career at Miami University with the same fifteen girls, and a dog. (Guess who brought the dog.) Now she's our office manager, scheduler, assistant with everything, two-day-old kitten raiser, and generally the one everyone wants to talk to about not just their pets but life, including their own illnesses.

She pulled into the parking lot on this Saturday to get her sons some new tennis shoes, but parked the car near the cages instead. There were animals to visit, and she was just the one to do it. There were a couple of women holding the leads of two forty-pound black dogs that were super friendly. There was a retriever mix who wanted a lot of attention, and a few dogs in cages back by the truck. After some petting of the front crew, Amy went back to see them. There were several yapping, hairy little guys, and a funny-looking white dog with a big head, a missing eye, and a bulldog bite sitting quietly in the back of his cage. He was the only one with a sign on his cage, and seemed a little scared.

Amy's sons Rob and Charlie went to get new tennis shoes, found some they liked, and got back in the Trailblazer. They all started for home, and when they were partway back to Hillsboro, Amy called my cell phone.

"Dad, there was the cutest dog this humane group had in a cage at the parking lot today. I think I'm in love. He sat in his cage with his big white ears sticking out at forty-five degree angles and looked so sad. He was reduced, and it made me sad too. He's white, about the size of a big Chihuahua, and perfect. What do you think?"

How do you answer that? "You better check with Matt." Asking your dad and asking your husband may get you two different answers. Matt was used to things like this, and his reply to Amy's constant talk of the white dog was, "Just think about it a while. I'm sure cooler heads and good judgment will prevail here."

She did think about it—all night long—and in the morning, with a perfectly cool head she called the leader of the adoption group and got directions to their facility. The next picture she texted to my phone was of a little white dog with a missing eye and an underbite, sitting in the back seat of Amy's car. Homer had found his home.

He spent his next few months socializing with his housemates, including a handsome bulldog, who was brought to the office for euthanasia because he couldn't be house-trained. They gave him to Amy instead, and said, "Good Luck!" Willie was living proof that God rarely gives both good looks and intelligence to the same being, and he *was* good-looking. His best pal was a tall, beautiful Doberman named Louise. A cat, who did his best to ignore the lot, sometimes walked over to him and sniffed. A congenial crew.

Then began a remarkable phenomenon. The Chamber of Commerce sent out fliers to all of its members soliciting "Cutest Baby" pictures. For fun, Amy sent in a picture of Homer in his best bowtie. He would wear any clothes you put on him and pose like a model, so portraits were a snap. He appeared on Facebook and holy cow, he won! Homer became the official Chamber "Spokesdog."

He was invited to the library for their summer reading program, "Every Hero Has a Story." He wore a Superdog cape and had his picture taken with kids, books, and library workers. He was all over Facebook.

Other business owners thought maybe Homer should come for a visit. After all, it was good advertising and fun too. For example, he went to our florist's and had a picture taken with a rose in his teeth and a bouquet behind him. Then he had a doughnut at the bakery in his cooking apron. He sat in the exam chair and had his funny teeth examined by a dentist, and wore his best jacket to have his eye examined by an optometrist in her office, and was then wearing a monocle in the next photo. Businesses called for appointments to have Homer dress up and be their "Spokes-dog." Facebook lit up with different Hillsboro business pictures featuring a one-eyed dog in fancy clothes. Homer attended the opening of every live performance at the Paxton Theater in Bainbridge, in his tuxedo of course. He attended a Reds game in Cincinnati, was photographed being held by Mr. Red, and was up on the Jumbotron several times. He went to Pups and Pucks Night at the Cincinnati Cyclones game and wore his Cyclones suit as he was held by the Cyclone himself. He even had a booth at the county fair where kids could have a "Picture with Homer" taken. He appeared at *sixty-four* businesses on his photo tour as Chamber Spokesdog, appearing with the owners of businesses as diverse as a floating bait shop and a national bourbon distillery. The little white dog with a unique face was recognizable all over town. Kids would yell out of car windows as Amy's family was stopped at a red light, "It's Homer! Hey, Homer!"

One night in Cincinnati a terrible thing happened. A police officer was chasing a bad guy and his K-9 unit was helping. As the dog brought the suspect down, the jerk pulled out a knife and stabbed him. We talked about this all morning at the office. For the past thirty-some years our office has taken care of the health of the city and county K-9 units. We called them Barney, Xena, Bronco, Asahn, Harley, Sando, Django, and Jorka, and really didn't think of them as "units" but as patients and friends. There were three active law enforcement K-9s in the county at this time. We knew them all, and didn't want anything like this to happen to them. So we used Homer's photo as a fundraiser, wearing a tiny police uniform as he posed with an actual K-9 unit in his real uniform, captioned: "Help Homer Help His Friends in Uniform." Over the course of several weeks, Homer raised over three thousand dollars in donations at the office and we bought three body-armor vests for our professional dogs in blue. Homer had power!

Why couldn't Homer's fame help other needy groups and not just dress up for fun? Amy had the idea of a line of t-shirts and sweatshirts with Homer's likeness. Dr. Reid Sharp was married to a graphic designer, Maddie Cupp, as luck would have it. She designed a Homer logo—a line drawing of Homer with big ears, an eye, and a wink, and a row of prominent lower teeth. Simple but absolutely Homer. The silkscreen work was easy, and before long the Homer clothing line was all over the streets of Highland County. He eventually appeared on calendars, tattoos, coffee mugs, beach bags, car magnets, hand fans, and wine glasses. The money he raised was given to local charities, local dog rescue groups, cystic fibrosis research, the Highland County Society for Children and Adults, Kamp Dovetail, developmental disabilities groups, and many others. He had his own Facebook and Instagram pages. He had the ability to be helpful in a big way.

The Festival of the Bells is a local three-day celebration uptown over the Fourth of July. We've had some big-name entertainment in our little town for this occasion, usually before their names were household words. Rascal Flatts, Brad Paisley, Taylor Swift, and many others have performed in past years to standing crowds that filled the uptown area. One of the three nights we have a gospel concert. It was hotter than hell at the gospel concert one year, so it was a good time to sell Homer hand fans. They were like the old funeral home fans, a cardboard fan on a flat stick, except the cardboard part was a silhouette of Homer's head, complete with a single eyehole you could look through—his logo. This human-powered wind-maker said, "I'm a Homer Fan," and the proceeds went to Kamp Dovetail. They sold out and that was a really good thing since one of Homer's favorite places to visit was Kamp Dovetail.

Every year Kamp Dovetail, a week-long outdoor camp for kids with developmental disabilities or serious handicaps, is held at Rocky Fork Lake State Park. The kids—and there are a lot of them—can camp, fish, play outdoor games, and generally do activities with other kids with similar problems, all with volunteer help. Homer would sit on wheelchairs all day long if you let him. The kids loved the little white dog, and couldn't wait to have him come and see them. One little boy with an eyepatch said, "Look! Homer's just like me!" Homer also made regular visits to schools, libraries, and youth groups, and was known by most of the kids in town.

Over the years he inspired artwork by artists as famous as Joe Smith, Nina Huryn, and at least thirty-one others. His portrait was done in oil on canvas, as wall hangings, as a huge mural, as Halloween art, and as a project for the high school art class. He never posed nude.

Someone submitted one of his photos as an entry in the "World's Cutest Mutt" contest, and one day Amy got a message in the mail that he had won. Of course.

Because of his work with businesses, public interest posts on Facebook, school visits, and his fundraising efforts for so many charities, Homer was named "Grand Marshal of the Christmas Parade" in Hillsboro. He rode in his Christmas outfit and hat, at the head of the parade on the top of an antique truck with sideboards announcing "Homer—Grand Marshal."

At home, Homer was just the dog who sat on Amy's husband Matt's lap while he watched Ohio State games. No one is famous at home. He had to be walked, fed, and vaccinated just like every other dog. One day he wasn't right. It seemed like he had trouble when he went out to "do his business." When your dad and brother are both veterinarians and you work with them daily, you have quick access to help. Homer had cancer. In spite of even more help from specialists, his tumor grew and Amy knew he wouldn't be with her much longer. When she realized that he was losing his fight, she let Homer go. He was fourteen.

Homer's death was announced on the Cincinnati television news that night. Each major channel had his picture, and a few of his accomplishments. Amy's last post on Facebook reminded everyone of his community contributions, and then made a last request.

It read, "So today our hearts are broken. I will miss my friend more than words can say. I will remind myself of 'how lucky I am to have something that makes saying goodbye so hard.' And please, one last time for Homer, make a holiday donation to your local animal shelter, or better yet, go adopt your new best friend."

I don't know how much was raised for other shelters, but in our office alone our clients donated enough that Amy was able to present a check for over seven thousand dollars to All Dogs Come From Heaven Rescue, the group that put Homer with Amy seven years earlier. They were surprised, and very thankful for such a gift in Homer's memory.

There are a lot of AKC breeders in the country with beautiful dogs of all shapes and sizes that will make great pets. You can find them easily on the internet. Maybe though, on your next hurried trip to town or the mall, there may be a group of people in a parking lot desperate to find homes for the ones that are harder to place. Maybe, sitting in a cage in the back, you may find your next best friend—a funny-looking little dog that no one wants. No one wanted Homer—he was reduced.

The More Things Change . . .

It's hard to go back to sleep when one wakes up at night and has a lot of worries. There was the dog in the kennel with the "chewing gum seizures" of distemper to think about. Did the medication stop the tremors or did the poor guy have a terrible night? There was the Philmore's cat that was kicked in the face by their cow. Their little girl was so worried about him. Still alive? The Schellings had an outbreak of a viral disease in their herd, and the state lab was no help so far. They were relying on him to stop their losses, and he'd thought about it for what seemed like hours.

And then the pandemic. Would his kids catch it, or his wife? He'd heard that several of his clients had it and a couple had died. The news didn't help. Half the country thought the politicians were overstepping their bounds with all the closings and restrictions. The other half thought the politicians weren't doing enough—we needed more closings and restrictions. The newspapers just made you upset. The pandemic was spreading out of control, and everyone was so tired of food shortages and crazy rules that even if you were allowed to go to church, you'd just pray for things to get back to normal. Government control was overwhelming. The bank wanted to be paid and no one could pay for a veterinarian.

He rolled over but it didn't help. He tried to make his mind blank—that might work, he thought. Then there was that damn woodpecker on the walnut tree out back—every morning at six. *Knockknockknock.* Why didn't his head explode?

He decided it was a lost cause, got out of bed, and got dressed to go to the office and check on the animals, especially the one with seizures. He went downstairs, had a glass of milk, and went out to the garage and wouldn't you know it—a flat tire. He pumped it up for the tenth time, climbed into his Model T, and left for the office. "You'd think by 1918 they could make a better tire than these junkers they put on!" And with that, Dr. Lukhart was on his way.

In 1849, a Frenchman named Karr gave us a familiar quotation: "The more things change, the more they stay the same." We look back a hundred years, hear the stories, and we think everything was different back then—but not really. Bill's dad practiced during World War I when food shortages were severe and life was tough in Hillsboro. They got through it, only to have the Spanish Flu pandemic hit the country. His practice survived and so did his family, but not without concern and sleepless nights.

There are plenty of nights when I've wondered about a patient at the office, and gotten out of bed to go over and check on it. There were times when I wondered if I could pay the bills, or stop a contagious outbreak at a farm, and just like Dr. Lukhart, in 1918, I couldn't sleep. And now there was the Coronavirus pandemic.

Oh, we have better diagnostic tools now. Reid can have a complete blood count and serum chemistry in his hands in twelve minutes. It took overnight or even two days for me to get this. My predecessor rarely used this bloodwork, and his dad never heard of it.

But on the other end of the lead, all four of us have had a worried client. This hasn't changed. "Will he be all right, Doc?" In 1912 and in 2021, the kid with the sick puppy looks at you the same way. The vehicles that vets drive are safer, faster, and better in every way, but the problems in the field remain constant. We know more about them now, but somebody still needs to put on some boots and deal with them. Someone needs to put on a gown and mask and operate on a problem to make the cat or dog well enough to go home. The kid's puppy needs to be fixed. The tools are better now, but the mechanic's job stays the same.

Adults sometimes ask schoolchildren, "What do you want to be when you grow up, kiddo?" In the top ten you'll hear, "A vet, because I love animals." As they got older, they usually ended up as a personnel manager, computer programmer, or high-school teacher.

But if you're an animal lover, at times the kid deep down inside comes back, and will remind you—once you thought that being able to fix someone's hurt cat, repair a dog that everyone thought would die, put the broken leg of the Kentucky Derby winner back together, or just be in a field with cattle all day would be terrific. It would.

I think if you'd walk into the office tomorrow and ask Dr. Reid Sharp, "Do you like your profession? Would you do anything else?" He would say the same thing now that I would have said when he was born, or Dr. Lukhart in 1938, or Dr. Lukhart's dad in 1912. "It's challenging most days. It's rewarding, and some days it will break your heart, but it will never be dull. I love it, and wouldn't consider doing anything else."

My wife says jokingly that I just pet dogs all day. It's true. I do get to spend a lot of time with animals, and I hope to continue for a while. I went to my fifty-year high school reunion, still in practice, and heard stories from my classmates about the fun they were having now that they've retired. They *finally* got to do what they wanted. I must have been retired all along!

One Last Thing . . .

In the seemingly endless months and years of the Coronavirus pandemic, we humans may have gotten a little "bad news weary." Who could we turn to for that? What's a good antidote for that?

Our animals. We may not have been able to hug our grandpa, but we could hug our golden retriever. Our cat still hopped on our bed in the morning, purring. Our Appaloosa waited for a trail ride, and she didn't need anyone's permission to go. Neither did our Red Heeler, who wanted to run along with his tongue out. Our pets and even our farm animals were unaffected by the global crisis, and gave us all the comfort they could. Your Lab could sit with you, watch the news and then look up and ask, "You gonna eat that?" Stuck at home with no one to socialize with but your dog, cat, chinchilla, or parrot? That's not so bad, is it?

In that terrible time we were given a coping mechanism that even in the worst of times, never fails. Our animals don't care if we're the mayor of a big city, the nurse on a bad ward, or the guy who lost his job and has it tough. They love us, will stick by us, and know something we sometimes forget: The most important thing in life is our family, and they will do all they can to be a part of it.

We're finally able to hug our grandma again. But luckily, we've always been able to hug our dog, feed our fish, ride our horse, bother our cat, and generally thank God for animals. They've always been and will always be our best friends.

Acknowledgments

There are quite a few people responsible for helping me bring these stories to you. I'm very grateful, and thank them here and now:

Rick Balkin, who acted as my literary agent until his retirement and was greatly responsible for seeing that my previous book was in print. He wasn't acknowledged properly back then, but I can thank him now. Thank you, sir!

Carol Cartaino, White Oak Editions. Frankly, without Carol's encouragement, creative editing, suggestions, and work as my agent, I would have never written a single word. In addition to being a longtime cat client, and the inspiration for two stories, she is a friend, and a great help to a lot of writers. Thank you, Carol!

Stephanie Hansen, owner and senior agent of Metamorphosis Literary Agency. Stephanie, as my representative to the publisher, bridged that gap between my computer and Lyons Press. Without her expertise, these stories would not be in your hands. Thank you, Stephanie!

I talked with Dick Lukens about retelling a few family stories about his grandfather, and he was encouraging and helpful. Dick is Bill's son, one of the three children of Dr. William L. Lukens and his wife Martha. Thanks, Dick.

Melissa Schelling, our Registered Animal Technician, who has worked at my right hand for forty-one years. She knows every client, helps every animal, and is faithful to her profession. She has been with me every day of my career. Thanks, Missy!

Susie, my wife. She's worked at the office, remembered helpful details about cases, proofread the stories, and added her own touches as we went along. We've been married over fifty years and we're hoping for fifty more. I'm so lucky! Thanks, Susie.

Our kids, Amy and Reid. I can't believe how lucky we are to have our kids grow up, go away to school, see some of the world, and then come back to Hillsboro. What a blast it is to work with them daily—they are such fun!

Our clients, not only for entrusting the care of their animals to us, but also for constantly asking when the next book would be out! They have a lot of patience, and are why practicing here is such a joy.

About the Author

Veterinarian **Robert T. Sharp**'s first book, *No Dogs in Heaven?*, was published to resounding critical acclaim, in both paperback and a special hardcover edition created by Barnes and Noble. It was also translated into Czech. An alert editor in New York read the book and asked him to write a monthly column—Ask a Country Vet—for the popular magazine *Country Living*. His expert and delightfully written answers to questions from readers across the country were read by millions during the five years he served as *Country Living*'s "country vet."

A lifelong Ohio resident, Rob received his AB in zoology and MA in aquatic ecology from Miami University in Oxford, Ohio. He served in the U.S. Air Force for the next five years as a KC-135 instructor/evaluator navigator with the 17th Bomb Wing of Strategic Air Command, and is a Vietnam veteran. He left the Air Force to attend The Ohio State University College of Veterinary Medicine, received his DVM degree in 1979, and has practiced in southern Ohio since graduation.

He married his hometown sweetheart and Miami alumna Susie Reid in 1970. They have two children: Amy, also a Miami University graduate, who works daily at the practice, and Reid, a graduate of Miami University and St. Georges University School of Veterinary Medicine. He received his DVM degree in 2012 and joined his dad in his practice in Hillsboro, Ohio.

Rob is a Presbyterian Elder, a Rotarian and Paul Harris Fellow, a member of the American Veterinary Medical Association, the Ohio Veterinary Medical Association, the Amateur Trapshooting Association, and the BMW Motorcycle Owners of America.

He and Susie live in a restored Victorian home in Hillsboro with a variety of animals.